What Holds Us Together

Reframing Addiction

Written By Aubrey Perin

What Holds Us Together: Reframing Addiction
Written by Aubrey Perin

Cover and interior design by Aubrey Perin
ISBN: 979-8-9988227-2-8
Second edition: 2026

For permissions or inquiries, contact:
Aubrey.i.perin@gmail.com

Printed in the United States of America

Contents

A Note on Repetition

Some words will return again and again in these pages.

That's not a mistake — it's a rhythm.

Addiction is repetition. Healing is repetition. And the return of familiar phrases isn't meant to convince you, but to hold you. To remind the body it is safe to come back to what it once needed to avoid.

If something shows up more than once, it's only because you might need to hear it more than once.

You are not being asked to race ahead. You are being invited to stay.

Introduction

What Holds Us Together

We don't spiral because we're weak.
We spiral because something broke — something inside us, something between us, something we once counted on to keep life from unraveling.

Addiction has long been framed as a problem to be fixed: a disease to manage, a behavior to eliminate, a failure of willpower or wiring. But those frames miss something vital. They miss the emotional logic that makes addiction feel, at least at first, like the only thing that works.

This book begins with a different assumption:
That addiction is not chaos, but coherence — a strategy to feel safe when nothing else holds.

We build rituals. We cling to patterns. We repeat behaviors that once brought us comfort or control. And when those rituals stop working, we don't just lose the behavior. We lose the emotional structure it held up. We lose the part of ourselves that still believed in relief.

And we grieve.

Most recovery models don't talk about that grief. They talk about stopping. Abstaining. Refraining. But very few ask:
What did this ritual mean to you?
What did it hold when nothing else could?

This book isn't about just breaking a habit. It's about understanding what made the habit necessary. It's about

1

the logic beneath the compulsion, the story behind the spiral, the quiet truth that sometimes — *sometimes* — addiction is the most honest response a person has to a world that never taught them how to hold themselves.

Whether you're here for yourself or for someone you love, you won't find shame in these pages. You'll find structure. Language. Permission.
You'll find a way to speak about what the behavior *meant*, not just what it did.
And you'll find the beginning of something new — not a return to who you were before the collapse, but a reconstruction of what might come after.

This is not a manual.
It's a reframing.
And a soft place to begin again.

Part I - Foundations

Before we talk about recovery, we have to talk about what's actually breaking.

Addiction has been defined in countless ways — as disease, as moral failure, as compulsion, as disorder. Each model offers something useful. But most leave something vital out. They explain what addiction does, but not *why it becomes necessary.*

They talk about behavior, but not about meaning. They study the symptoms, but rarely ask what the ritual is trying to hold.

This section is about returning to the beginning — not the beginning of the behavior, but the emotional architecture that made the behavior make sense. It's about seeing addiction not as chaos, but as coherence. A strategy. A rhythm. A fragile but brilliant attempt to regulate what was never safely held by others.

Here, we'll explore what addiction is *before* it collapses. What it gives us. Why it works — until it doesn't. We'll talk about patterns, rituals, and the quiet logic that drives repetition. We'll examine how addiction both protects and performs. And we'll begin to ask a different kind of question:

Not *"Why can't I stop?"*
But *"What was I trying to hold together?"*

These are the foundations — not of the behavior, but of the person beneath it. The person who was never trying to escape.
Just trying to stay intact.

Chapter 1 - What Addiction Really Is

Addiction has been defined so many times, in so many ways, that the word itself feels worn thin — like something passed around too often, touched too carelessly. We call it a disease. A disorder. A moral failing. A genetic inheritance. A behavioral compulsion. Sometimes, all at once.

These definitions don't always disagree — but they rarely go far enough. Most name the *what* but avoid the *why*. They explain the mechanism, not the meaning. And meaning matters, because addiction is never just a behavior. It's a story — and most of the time, it's the only story that ever made someone feel safe.

We say addiction hijacks the brain. That it rewires reward centers, disrupts decision-making, destroys logic. And maybe it does. But long before it does that, addiction does something else:

It works.

At least at first.
It offers stillness where there was chaos.
It offers rhythm where there was only noise.
It offers *something* — when nothing else has.

If you've ever been in it — truly in it — you know this. You know the relief that came with the first drink, the first scroll, the first hit, the first lie that landed just right and bought you one more day of not falling apart. You know how precious that moment was — not because it made you feel good, but because it made you feel *intact*.

That's the part the traditional models miss. Addiction isn't just about compulsion or craving. It's about coherence. It's about holding yourself together when nothing else will.

And that's why it's so hard to let go.

Pause and Consider
What if it was never about stopping?
What if the real question was: what held you together before this stopped working?

The disease model — the most widely accepted in modern treatment — offers compassion in place of blame. It tells people they aren't bad, they're sick. It medicalizes suffering. That's not nothing. In fact, for many, it's a lifesaving shift. But it also does something else: it turns the person into a patient. It pathologizes the spiral without honoring the emotional blueprint behind it. It says: you're malfunctioning — here's the treatment.

But what if the "malfunction" was an adaptation?
What if the behavior was a precise emotional strategy — developed, repeated, refined — not to escape life, but to survive it?

The moral model is worse — but more familiar. It whispers in churches, courtrooms, family kitchens: You could stop if you wanted to. You're choosing this. You're weak. Selfish. Shameful.

But anyone who's lived in the spiral knows — if it were about *wanting* to stop, most of us would've done so a long time ago.

What we wanted was to stop hurting.

And the only way we knew to do that was to repeat the pattern that used to work — even when it didn't anymore.

There's a subtle cruelty in the language of "choice." It implies clarity, logic, distance from the thing. But addiction doesn't happen at a distance. It happens inside the body, the breath, the nervous system. It's not an idea you consider. It's a ritual your whole being leans into — often before your conscious mind has caught up.

What traditional models call dysfunction, I call devotion. Not to the substance, but to the pattern. To the ritual. To the fragile logic of *if I do this, I won't fall apart.*

This book isn't here to replace existing models. It's here to deepen them. To remind us that underneath the compulsion is often a grief that was never named. A loneliness that was never held. A version of safety that had to be built in secret because no one else knew how to offer it.

Addiction, in this light, is not a character flaw. It's not even a disease.

It's the last honest system standing in the aftermath of emotional collapse.

And when we understand that — when we see addiction not as defiance but as design — we can begin to ask a better question:

Not "Why won't they stop?"

But "What were they trying to hold together?"

1.1

The Limits of the Current Models

We've gotten good at describing addiction. We know what it does to the body, to relationships, to memory. We know how it looks when it spirals — what it costs, who it hurts. But for all that description, most models still miss the most essential question:

What was the behavior protecting?

Because addiction isn't just a pattern to eliminate. It's a system someone built — often with care, often in crisis — to keep themselves from falling apart.

The dominant models each offer a frame, but most stop at the surface. The disease model was, in its time, a revolution. It told us that addiction wasn't about bad choices or moral failure. It gave people permission to step out of shame and into treatment. And for many, that reframe saved lives.

But it also did something else: it pathologized the ritual. It turned the person into a patient, their pain into a diagnosis. It invited compassion, yes — but often at the cost of curiosity. It asked, *What's wrong with you?* instead of *What happened to you?* or *What held you together before this was the only thing that did?*

Then there's the moral model — still alive in courtrooms, families, and Facebook comment threads. It whispers that addiction is a choice. That suffering is the consequence of weakness, selfishness, indulgence. It tells people that if they *really* wanted to stop, they would. That they just haven't hit bottom hard enough yet.

But ask anyone who's been there — really been there — and they'll tell you:
If it were about wanting to stop, we would have.
We wanted to stop *hurting*.
We just didn't know how to feel safe without the pattern that used to work.

Even the behavioral model, which aims to neutralize addiction by treating it as habit, as operant conditioning, as reward-based repetition — misses the mark when it forgets that the "reward" wasn't pleasure. It was *regulation*. It was the feeling of being okay, even if only for a moment. A feeling that, for some, never existed before the behavior arrived.

Each of these models offers insight. But insight without intimacy can feel cold. It explains the compulsion without acknowledging the sacredness of what the person was trying to hold together.

Addiction is rarely about thrill-seeking. It's about coherence-seeking. It's not a break from logic — it *is* logic. The kind you write in the dark when no one's coming to help, when the pain is louder than the room, and when the only thing that ever seemed to work is the thing you're now being told to give up.

None of these models are entirely wrong. But none of them ask enough.

They don't ask what the behavior *meant*.
They don't ask what the person would be losing — not just giving up — if they let it go.

And so, treatment becomes a story of removal. Not restoration.

But what if the goal wasn't to stop the behavior as fast as possible?
What if it was to understand what the behavior was holding — and begin, gently, to build something else that could hold just as well?

That's where this book begins.
Not at the point of diagnosis — but at the moment the pattern stopped working.
At the edge of grief, where most models end — and where, I believe, healing should begin.

1.2

The Emotional Logic of Addiction

Addiction, at its core, is not about getting high. It's about getting *still*.
It's about finding a moment — however brief, however costly — where the chaos inside you finally quiets. Where the room feels less sharp. Where the noise settles enough to remember what breathing feels like.

That's the part so often missed: the internal function.
Addiction isn't just a behavior. It's a system.
It's an emotional architecture built in the absence of safety, stability, or care. It begins as rhythm — not recklessness. As relief — not rebellion.

This is what I call the emotional logic of addiction.

It doesn't matter whether the ritual is drinking, scrolling, bingeing, restricting, gambling, running, or clinging to a relationship that hurts. The content varies. But the pattern stays the same:

"When I do this, I feel okay."
"When I do this, I know who I am."
"When I do this, I don't have to feel everything else."

This is not chaos. It is survival.
And the logic is consistent — often *more* consistent than the environments the person grew up in.

Most people don't become addicted because they enjoy losing control.
They become addicted because they've *never* felt in control — not emotionally, not relationally, not existentially. The behavior steps in as a kind of anchor: a way to locate themselves in space and time when nothing else gives shape to their experience.

That's why it becomes so hard to let go.
Not because of chemical dependency alone, but because the behavior *worked*.
It made sense. It made *you* make sense — in a world that never explained itself and often punished you for asking.

————————

Pause and Consider
What if the ritual made more sense than the world around you?
What if it was never about pleasure, but about precision — your last working formula for not falling apart?

There is a kind of sacredness to the early rituals of addiction. A cup placed in the same cabinet. A walk taken at the same hour. A silence you protect with routine. At first, it doesn't feel dangerous. It feels… stabilizing. Gentle. Predictable.

But emotional logic is not the same as emotional safety. Just because something works doesn't mean it will keep working. And when the return begins to fade — when the ritual loses its power — the pain it once held starts to leak.

That's when repetition becomes compulsion.
Not because the person is failing — but because they're trying to recover the feeling the ritual used to provide.

They pour a second drink, not out of indulgence, but out of grief:
"Why didn't the first one work?"

They binge again, not because they want to, but because it's the only thing that ever *stopped* the spiral.
They isolate not because they don't need others, but because they don't know how to need safely.

This is the emotional logic that underlies the spiral.
It's not irrational. It's *exactly* rational — for a system that was never taught how to regulate, contain, or express its full humanity.

Addiction begins where coherence ends.
And until something else steps in to hold that pain, the ritual will keep trying to do the job.

1.3

Coherence Over Chaos

Addiction is rarely the first problem. More often, it's the first solution that worked. It arrives not as a storm, but as a structure — a way to survive the storm when everything else stops making sense. And yet, from the outside, addiction is almost always described as disorder: chaotic, reckless, destructive. It's framed as an unraveling. But if you look closer, what you often see isn't chaos at all. You see control. You see a person clinging to the one thing in their life that follows a pattern.

That pattern might be physical — a repeated behavior, a familiar cycle. But beneath the surface, it's emotional. It is an attempt to regulate experience, to contain overwhelm, to make sense of feelings that no one ever taught them to hold. What looks like self-destruction is often self-preservation in its most distilled form. The ritual, whatever shape it takes, functions as an internal scaffolding — a system of meaning and emotional containment built in the absence of safer ones.

This is what I mean when I say addiction is coherence, not chaos. It is a system of internal order, one often constructed with extraordinary intelligence in response to early instability, trauma, or chronic mis-attunement. The drink, the pill, the game, the scroll — these are not inherently meaningful. But their repetition, their predictability, becomes symbolic. If the ritual works, the person knows who they are. They know what comes next. They are no longer lost in the noise.

Even when the behavior begins to harm them, it still serves that organizing function. And that is what makes it so difficult to dismantle. The addicted person is not clinging to a pleasure. They are clinging to a pattern that once kept them from falling apart. If we miss that — if we only see the symptom and not the system — we miss the humanity inside the habit. We risk telling people to give up the only thing that made their world feel stable, without offering them something stronger to take its place.

There is an emotional precision to addiction that deserves to be understood. It is not erratic. It is exact — calibrated over time, repeated for good reason, and deeply personal in the way it holds what could not otherwise be held. To treat addiction only as disorder is to ignore the logic that made it necessary. And if we ignore that logic, we cannot possibly build something that will replace it. We end up asking people to recover without recognizing what they are recovering *from* — or *into*.

Coherence is what the person was always seeking. Not excitement, not numbness, not escape. Just a sense that their feelings make sense. That their life has rhythm. That they can count on something — even if that something is slowly undoing them. Until we understand that drive, we will continue to misread the spiral as failure, when in truth, it is a ritual that's trying to hold back collapse.

Vignette: The Porch Light

Every night before bed, he checked the porch light.

Even when it wasn't his job. Even when it had already been checked. Even when he lived alone and there was no one left to forget.

It wasn't about safety, not really. The neighborhood was quiet. The motion sensor worked fine. But still, he'd walk to the front door, peer out through the side window, and make sure the light was on.

At first, it was a habit — one passed down from his father, who always said a lit porch made a home feel "ready." But after the divorce, after the house got quieter, the ritual changed. It stopped being about the outside. It became about him.

Because when the porch was dark, the house felt abandoned.
And when the light was on, it meant someone was still trying.

Some nights, he'd turn it off just to turn it back on again — a little ceremony to reset the feeling that he had lost control of the day.
On nights when the loneliness pressed in, he'd linger by the door, looking at the light like it was proof that he was still here. Still holding. Still worth illuminating.

Eventually, the habit grew. He began checking it at dinner, then again before brushing his teeth. On especially hard days, he'd sit in the car before coming inside and stare at the bulb for a moment longer than necessary, waiting for something inside to steady.

No one ever asked about it. No one knew it mattered.

But to him, that single ritual — that quiet confirmation that the world outside was still lit, still visible, still responding — was the last thing that made him feel like the night wouldn't swallow him whole.

He couldn't explain why it mattered. Only that it did.

And later, when the bulb burned out and he forgot to replace it, the spiral came quietly. Not in some dramatic collapse — just a slow drift. Later nights. Unwashed dishes. Missed texts. A kind of heaviness that returned without permission.

It took him weeks to notice that everything had started slipping the day the light went dark.

Not because the bulb failed.
But because the rhythm broke.
And with it, the last pattern that had ever made him feel like the day still belonged to him.

Pause and Consider

What routines do you engage in without thinking?
What moments — however small — help you feel like the day still belongs to you?
Could some of those rituals be emotional anchors, quietly keeping you upright when words or logic can't?

And if one of them disappeared… would anyone know it mattered?

1.4

Why This Frame Matters

It's easy to mistake this reframing of addiction as soft — as something that risks excusing harm or over-complicating what many believe should be simple: just stop. But understanding addiction as coherence is not about sympathy at the cost of accountability. It's about giving addiction the precision it deserves. It's about replacing the language of judgment and disorder with a more accurate emotional map — one that can guide someone not just away from the behavior, but toward something that might actually hold.

When we see addiction as an emotional survival strategy — a system built for stability, not indulgence — we begin to ask better questions. Not "How do I get this person to stop?" but "What held them together before this?" "What do they lose if they let it go?" "What else can offer that same sense of containment, identity, and rhythm?"

These questions are not distractions from recovery — they are the foundation. Because no one lets go of something that made them feel safe without knowing what will hold them next. And that is where most systems fall short. They remove the behavior without replacing the structure. They interrupt the spiral without recognizing that the spiral *was* the structure — the only one that ever made sense.

When we miss the meaning beneath the behavior, we risk doing harm even in our efforts to help. We tell people they're broken, or diseased, or dangerous. We ask them to surrender rituals that once saved their lives without offering them new ways to feel alive. And we wonder why they return to the pattern. But of course they do. Of course they would. Anyone would. Because the alternative isn't just absence — it's emotional freefall.

This frame matters because it doesn't just name the problem. It humanizes the process. It gives people language for what they were doing — not just what they were avoiding. And in that language, there is dignity. There is structure. There is a way forward that doesn't begin with blame or end in erasure.

Addiction is not the opposite of willpower. It is what willpower looks like when someone is trying to survive with no other tools. It is not a defect. It is design — one built under pressure, under grief, under silence. And like all designs, it can be revised. But only if we understand what it was originally built to protect.

In the chapters ahead, we won't focus on how to stop the pattern. We'll focus on how it was formed — and what might take its place when stopping becomes possible. Before we talk about collapse, we need to talk about ritual. Because most addiction doesn't begin with a breakdown. It begins with something that once worked.

Chapter 2 - Ritual Before Ruin

Addiction doesn't begin with crisis. It begins with pattern.

Before the spiral, before the breakdown, before the behavior becomes something to hide — there is rhythm. Something consistent. Something comforting. A ritual that works, until it doesn't.

And for a time, that ritual is sacred. Not in a religious sense, but in the way it orders experience. It offers a symbolic contract: *If I do this, I'll feel okay.* Whether it's the quiet of a morning walk, the pop of a bottle cap, the glow of a screen late at night — the ritual holds meaning beyond the act itself. It becomes a kind of emotional shorthand: a way to reset, to return, to remember who you are.

For some, that ritual begins with celebration. For others, with survival. But what links all rituals that give way to addiction is not how they start, but how precisely they serve the self before the collapse. The behavior doesn't feel compulsive in the beginning. It feels stabilizing. Grounding. Necessary. It fits neatly into a personal equation: *If I do this, then I know what comes next.*

And it's not always unhealthy. Many rituals are life-affirming. They help us navigate uncertainty, contain emotion, transition between identities. Lighting a candle before bed. Touching the doorknob twice before leaving the house. Putting on the same playlist to cook dinner. These aren't just habits — they are ways of marking time, signaling safety, shaping identity. They are the scaffolding on which a life is quietly built.

But for someone who was never taught how to regulate emotion relationally — who had to build their own system of coherence in the absence of safety, support, or structure — the ritual becomes more than helpful. It becomes *essential*. The only working part of a system too fragile to risk change.

That's where addiction begins: in the space where ritual becomes the only way to feel whole.

When something interrupts that ritual — when a person loses the job, the relationship, the identity that made the behavior feel safe — the structure begins to break. But rather than let go, the person clings harder. Not because they're unaware of the damage, but because they remember what the ritual used to provide.

The world might see dependence. But the person inside the pattern sees devotion. Not to the substance, but to the coherence it once promised. And until we understand that devotion — until we recognize what the ritual was actually doing — we will continue to misunderstand what's really at stake when we ask someone to stop.

To understand addiction, we must begin with the ritual. Not the wreckage it caused, but the rhythm it offered.

Because before there was ruin, there was relief.
And that's where the real story starts.

2.1

The Function of Ritual

Ritual is how we make the world make sense. It is how we move from moment to moment with some sense of orientation — a story about what comes next, even when the page is blank. For many, ritual is protective. Not because the act itself is magical, but because the repetition creates rhythm, and rhythm creates safety.

The human nervous system thrives on rhythm. Breath, heartbeat, speech, light. We organize ourselves through cycles, through sequences. Ritual is one of the oldest tools we have for emotional regulation — a way to hold the unknown within the familiar. Lighting a candle before a prayer. Tapping the steering wheel three times before turning the key. Standing in a particular place while brushing your teeth. These small patterns aren't superstitions — they're anchors. They mark space. They signal order. They hold chaos at the door.

In healthy contexts, rituals are relational. They happen in shared meals, community traditions, cultural ceremonies, or simply in the quiet cadence between people who know how to stay soft with one another. But when those systems fail — when there is no community, no containment, no safe parent or partner or place to return to — ritual becomes internalized. It moves from the collective to the private, from symbolic gesture to emotional necessity.

For the person who grew up without emotional attunement, ritual isn't optional. It's survival. It's the only way to feel like they still belong to something — even if that "something" is as simple as a cigarette after lunch or the sequence of shows they fall asleep to at night. It's not about the substance. It's not about entertainment. It's about the predictability of experience — a self-generated rhythm that creates enough coherence to move through another day.

These rituals don't raise alarm at first. Often, they look benign — a walk, a playlist, a glass of wine, a Sunday routine. They may even be praised. But for the person whose internal world feels fragile, these rituals are doing more than they appear. They aren't just helping the day feel smoother — they're holding grief. Containing fear. Masking shame. They are quiet mechanisms for emotional survival, invisible to almost everyone except the person who needs them most.

And they work.
Until they don't.

2.2

When Ritual Becomes Regulation

There's a quiet line that separates ritual from regulation. It doesn't announce itself. It doesn't arrive all at once. It drifts in — slowly, silently — until the gesture that once brought calm now carries weight. And that weight becomes the whole point.

In the beginning, the ritual feels like choice. You take the walk. You open the drink. You queue the show or scroll the feed or call the same person at the same time of day. These are small things — easy things. They give shape to transition, offer comfort in repetition. They're not problems. They're patterns. And patterns feel good. They make the world manageable.

But for the emotionally unanchored — for the person who carries grief without language, shame without witness, pain without a name — the ritual doesn't just soothe. It starts to *hold*. And once a ritual becomes a primary container for emotional regulation, it stops being optional. It becomes a condition of stability. A personal infrastructure: silent, sacred, and brittle.

The behavior doesn't need to escalate to become essential. Sometimes it stays small — just more frequent, more rigid. You don't just take the walk; you *have* to. You don't just enjoy the glass of wine; you *need* it to exhale. The show you used to watch out of joy now plays on repeat because the silence is unbearable. You don't even notice the shift at first. You just know that skipping the ritual feels worse than doing it.

That's the threshold where autonomy begins to erode. Not because the person is weak — but because they've outsourced their emotional regulation to a behavior. And often, it's the only behavior that works.

No one taught them how to self-soothe without it. No one modeled how to move through overwhelm with support. And the world rarely offers language for the internal choreography of survival. So the ritual becomes sacred. Protected. Repeated. And slowly, invisibly, it becomes a rule.

You follow the rule because it keeps you from unraveling. And even when you see it tightening — even when you know the rule is starting to rule you — letting go doesn't feel like freedom. It feels like collapse.

Because the ritual doesn't just regulate the body. It regulates the story. It says, *You're okay now. You know how this goes. You're still in control.*

Which is why its erosion feels like a threat.
Not to pleasure.
To coherence.

Vignette: The Gym Bag

He packed his gym bag every night before bed.

It was a simple routine. Shirt, shorts, socks, shoes, protein bar. Always in the same order. Always on the left side of the couch. He told himself it helped him stay disciplined. That it kept his mornings focused. That it was good for him — and it was, at first.

After the divorce, after the awkward silences at work, after the phone calls he stopped returning, the gym became his constant. It was the place where his body made sense, where he could count reps instead of feelings, where he could sweat instead of speak. No one asked him to explain anything there. No one noticed the bags under his eyes or the way he avoided eye contact in the locker room. The gym didn't ask questions. It just opened.

Over time, the gym bag became a ritual. Packing it meant tomorrow still had shape. Laying it on the couch meant the day wasn't over yet — it was just pausing. He never questioned it. It was part of the routine.

But then he skipped a day. A flat tire, a late meeting, something small. And he felt it — the tremor beneath his skin, the sudden pressure in his chest. That night, he couldn't sleep. His heart raced. He snapped at the drive-thru worker for forgetting his straw. Everything felt louder. Off-kilter. He couldn't explain it, except to say that something was *wrong*.

The next morning, he doubled his workout. Then he did it again the day after that. He told himself he was just getting back on track.

He didn't see the shift. Didn't notice that the gym bag had become more than a habit — it had become a condition. A rule. Not going didn't just make him restless. It made him question everything. Whether he was slipping. Whether he was still in control. Whether he was still okay.

And deeper than that — though he couldn't say it out loud — it made him wonder if he had ever been enough to begin with.

He told himself it was about discipline, but when he missed a day, the old shame crept back in. The questions he thought he'd outrun at the bench press returned in whispers. Maybe if he'd been more committed. More toned. Less tired. Maybe she wouldn't have left. Maybe he would've been worth staying for.

He packed the bag not just to prepare for tomorrow — but to outrun a past that still haunted him. The divorce. The failure, *his* failure. The quiet sense that no matter how many times he showed up, he was still one skipped workout away from being unlovable.

The gym bag had become more than routine. It was a barrier between him and collapse. Between the self he performed and the self he still didn't know how to comfort. Without it, the night stretched out too long. The silence too wide. The ache too close.

And so, he kept packing.
Not for fitness.
But for coherence.
Because if he stopped — even for a day — everything might fall apart.

2.3

The Moment It Changes

The moment the ritual stops working doesn't always feel dramatic. Sometimes, it's not even noticeable. There's no crisis, no explosion. Just a flicker. A hesitation. A feeling that the old rhythm didn't land quite right — that the usual thing didn't bring its usual relief.

It could be a sip that doesn't calm the nerves. A scroll that feels hollow. A run that ends in exhaustion instead of release. The behavior hasn't changed, but the return has. What once brought stillness now stirs up something unsettled. The body finishes the ritual, but the relief doesn't come. And for a second — maybe longer — the person wonders if something's wrong.

But they don't call it collapse. Not yet.

Instead, they repeat the pattern. That's what the system was built to do. If one drink doesn't work, maybe two. If one loop through the feed doesn't help, maybe a second... A third. If the silence still hurts, turn the volume up louder. The logic isn't broken — it's just... resisting. That's what they tell themselves. That's what they need to believe.

Because if the ritual no longer holds, what will?

This is the beginning of the spiral — not when things get worse externally, but when the internal equation begins to crack. The person isn't just chasing a feeling. They're chasing *order*. The ritual used to bring it. Now it doesn't. And instead of slowing down to grieve that loss, they speed up. Not out of recklessness — but out of desperation to retrieve the structure that made the world feel survivable.

That's the paradox. From the outside, the behavior looks more chaotic. But from the inside, the person is trying harder than ever to stay coherent. The rituals become more rigid, more frequent, more sacred — not because they're working, but because they're not. And when the behavior finally collapses under its own weight, the person doesn't just feel lost.

They feel betrayed.

The one thing that ever made them feel okay is gone. And in its place: shame, confusion, and the slow realization that they have no backup plan. No internal scaffolding. No map. Just grief. And silence. And the unbearable question they've avoided all along:

What now?

Pause and Consider

If this chapter brought up something heavy, take a breath. You don't need to explain it. You don't need to justify how it began or defend how it's held you.

You built something that worked. That's not failure. That's brilliance.

The patterns you relied on — they weren't wrong. They were yours. They were how you made it through. They made sense in the world you came from.

If they're starting to falter now, that doesn't mean *you're* falling apart. It means you're beginning to feel what the pattern protected you from. That's not collapse. That's contact. That's the beginning of something true.

You don't have to give anything up yet. You don't have to fix or solve or change.

Just notice. Just feel. Just stay.

That is enough for now.

You are not alone in this.

If you've come this far, I trust you're ready to look at the pattern with me — not as shame, but as structure.

Chapter 3 - The Game of Addiction

Addiction is often described as private — something hidden, something solitary, something people do when no one is looking. But that's only half the story.

The other half is performance.

Most people living inside addiction don't disappear from the world entirely. They manage jobs, families, conversations, errands. They show up. They smile. They play the part. And while the behavior may happen in secret, the *management* of it is often public. Not in obvious ways, but in careful ones. They avoid questions. They reroute suspicion. They stay one step ahead of the collapse. They get good at it — so good, in fact, that sometimes even they believe the act.

This is the game of addiction.

Not because it's manipulative or shallow — but because it has rules. Roles. Rituals. Whether conscious or not, the person begins to navigate the world through a set of internalized strategies: how to keep people close without letting them in, how to stay visible without becoming vulnerable, how to look functional when they feel anything but.

Some play the game socially — by being funny, productive, useful, needed. Some play it alone — by building tight, repetitive worlds where nothing interrupts the ritual. Most do both. They switch modes depending on the space they're in, the people they're with, the version of themselves they need to protect.

And beneath it all, they follow rules. Not laws written on paper, but private rules shaped by pain: *Don't ask for help. Don't let anyone see the worst of it. Don't stop performing — or everything might fall apart.*

This chapter is about those rules.
The ones we never agreed to but still obey.
The ones that shape how addiction shows up in us — and what it means to begin letting go.

3.1

The Social Mode

Addiction doesn't just live in solitude. It thrives in relationship — both with others and with identity. The social mode isn't a single experience. It has layers. Sometimes it's personal, invisible — a strategy to stay coherent in public. Other times, it's cultural — shared language, behavior, and rhythm that masks the same pain through group ritual.

These two perspectives can seem opposite, but they share the same purpose: preserving coherence in a context where direct vulnerability feels impossible.

3.1a

The Social Mode

Addiction doesn't always look like withdrawal. Sometimes, it looks like the person who's always "on." The one who shows up early. The one who remembers your birthday. The one with the sharp joke, the big laugh, the ability to hold the room just long enough to keep anyone from asking how they're doing.

This is the social mode of addiction — a strategy for managing perception, protecting coherence, and deflecting inquiry. It's not about deception. It's about survival. It's the act of holding yourself together in public, even as something inside is quietly beginning to splinter.

People in the social mode are often praised. They seem high-functioning, dependable, generous. They're the caregivers. The performers. The fixers. They rarely ask for help. They rarely say they're struggling. Because the performance isn't just for others — it's for themselves. If they can manage their image, if they can stay in control, maybe they'll feel okay.

The social mode often begins early. For many, it was learned in childhood — the art of reading a room, of anticipating needs, of becoming who others needed them to be before they even had words for their own needs. That skill becomes a mask. Not because it's fake, but because it's incomplete. It shows the part that earns love. It hides the part that holds pain.

And behind that mask, the ritual continues. Sometimes quietly — an extra drink before the party, a pill to smooth the edges, a secret routine to make the public self more bearable. Sometimes more visibly — bingeing and overcompensating in cycles, retreating and returning with just enough energy to reset the performance.

But the effort is exhausting. Because the person isn't just managing their addiction — they're managing how others experience them. They're holding two identities at once: the one that performs, and the one that's barely hanging on. And they fear that if the performance slips, everything will unravel.

It's easy to overlook someone in the social mode. To believe they're fine because they smile. To praise their resilience while missing their collapse. But sometimes the people who hold it together best are the ones in the most pain — because holding it together *is* their addiction. It's not just what they do.

It's who they think they have to be.

3.1b

Belonging Through Behavior: Group Ritual as Cover

Addiction doesn't always isolate. Sometimes it binds. In the social mode, addiction becomes embedded in group dynamics. Drinking at bars, group gambling, party culture, obsessive workout communities, even high-control social media spaces — all create environments where the addictive behavior is not only normalized, but ritualized.

The group provides a script, a rhythm, and — most importantly — a shared language for regulation. Within these social rituals, the individual no longer has to explain their behavior. It is woven into the culture. It's expected. It's rewarded. The behavior becomes a social mask, allowing participants to appear functional, connected, even enthusiastic — while still preserving the underlying ritual that sustains them.

For individuals who mask heavily in daily life — such as autistic, codependent, or trauma-impacted people — this shared behavioral ritual offers cover. Eccentricities can be blamed on the alcohol, the high, the hustle. Emotional distance becomes fatigue, intensity becomes charisma. These rituals create plausible deniability, allowing people to be emotionally dysregulated in socially acceptable ways.

But the coherence found in these environments is often conditional. If the behavior shifts — or if the person tries to leave the group — the connection disappears. Relationships that once felt authentic are revealed to be dependent on participation. The ritual was the bond. And when it breaks, the person is left with both their original pain and a fresh grief: the grief of disappearing from a place they thought they belonged.

Pause and Consider

What if addiction isn't just a personal problem — but a cultural one?

What if the very behaviors we question in ourselves are the same ones we celebrate in the spaces around us — the hustle, the binge, the always-on, the "just one more"?

In Western culture, we often confuse intensity with connection. We turn rituals of survival into performances of identity. We pour ourselves into work, into wellness, into wine, into productivity, into screens — and we call it normal, even admirable.

But normalization doesn't mean nourishment.

Just because something is accepted doesn't mean it's safe. Just because something is shared doesn't mean it's sacred.

This isn't about blame. It's about noticing.

Because when we name the system, we start to understand that our pain didn't begin inside us — it began in the environments that shaped us. And healing doesn't just mean changing ourselves.

It means questioning what we were taught to call healthy.

3.2

The Solitary Mode

There is a quietness to the solitary mode that can feel almost sacred. No applause. No audience. Just the ritual and the person it was built to hold.

This is where addiction becomes pure — not in intensity, but in intimacy. The repetition, the rhythm, the control. No one needs to understand it. No one needs to agree with it. It doesn't have to be explained, justified, or performed. It simply *is*.

The solitary mode isn't defined by isolation alone — it's defined by the absence of interruption. No outside voices. No accountability. No reflective surfaces. Just the self and the behavior, locked in a feedback loop where the only language that makes sense is the one the pattern speaks.

This isn't escapism in the dismissive sense.
It's escape in the architectural sense — a construction designed to contain emotional volatility. Drinking alone. Binge-watching. Compulsive eating. Obsessive gaming. Isolated sexual rituals. These aren't random or indulgent. They're precise. They reduce the world to a single variable: the behavior. And within that narrow frame, there is relief. Not because it heals anything — but because it prevents everything else from spilling in.

In this way, solitary addiction simulates control. It gives the person a place where nothing unpredictable can touch them. Where they are no longer vulnerable to the chaos outside — or to the messiness of relationships, memory, grief. Within the ritual, there is still rhythm. Still regulation. Still coherence — even if it comes at a cost.

And the cost is dissociation.

Because the behavior is private, it becomes harder to interrupt. Harder to see clearly. Without the reinforcement of social witnessing, the lines begin to blur. It becomes easier to lie to oneself, easier to confuse momentary stillness with sustainable healing. And over time, the ritual doesn't just protect the person from the outside world — it begins to replace the inside one.

The person no longer drinks.
They are a drinker.
They don't just run.
They are a runner.
They don't just isolate.
They are someone who "just prefers to be alone."

This is how the game becomes identity. The ritual stops being a behavior and starts becoming a definition. And in a world where emotional incoherence is punished, being legible — even falsely — feels safer than being honest.

But identity built around ritual must be constantly maintained. And when the ritual begins to crack — when it no longer delivers the coherence it once promised — the person is left without a framework. Without rhythm. Without relief.

What began as a structure becomes a trap.
And what began as a game becomes a question of survival.

Vignette: The After-Party

He used to drink with friends. Loud bars, crowded porches, tailgates before games. It felt electric — chaotic in the best way. Everyone laughing too hard. Music always too loud. He was the one who brought the bottle, poured the shots, toasted nothing at all. They called him fun. Reliable. The guy who always had a plan for Friday night.

In those days, drinking meant people. It meant rhythm. It meant knowing who he was — the guy who could take the edge off the room and hold it there, just long enough for everyone to feel okay. No one asked how he was doing. They didn't have to. He looked like he was thriving.

Eventually, people changed. They settled down. Got jobs with early mornings. Started skipping the bar, started slowing down. But he didn't. The party got smaller. First five people. Then two. Then none. He started drinking at home, telling himself it was just easier that way — no lines, no noise, no Uber. Just comfort.

At first, it didn't feel different. The same brand. The same pour. The same playlist. But something shifted. There was no one left to laugh with. No one to mirror his energy. No ritual of clinking glasses or leaning too close. The rhythm was still there — but the connection was gone.

He stopped pouring for others.
And started measuring only for himself.

It wasn't about celebration anymore. It was about stillness. Predictability. Silence. The drink became a doorway — not to joy, but to quiet. To forgetting. To stopping the thoughts that wouldn't shut off at night. And the man who once lit up the room now drank with the lights off, the volume low, the phone on silent.

No one called him "fun" anymore. But no one asked if he was okay, either.

He still poured the same drink. Still followed the same ritual. But the meaning had changed.
The behavior stayed the same.
The context collapsed.
And the person he had performed was gone.

All that remained was the glass, the silence, and the ache that came when the buzz wore off too early.

Pause and Consider

Sometimes, the behavior doesn't change — but everything around it does.

What once felt like connection slowly becomes containment. What once brought energy now only brings silence. You're still following the same steps… but the meaning is gone.

That shift is easy to miss. Especially when the ritual still works just enough to keep going. But under the repetition, something inside is grieving — not just the behavior, but the version of you that made sense when others were watching.

If you're noticing that the same pattern no longer brings the same relief, that's not failure.

That's awareness. That's clarity.

It might even be the beginning of your return.

You were never meant to carry this alone.
And the person you were inside the ritual? They're still here — waiting to be seen without the script.

3.3

Switching Between Modes

Addiction rarely lives in just one place. Most people don't fit neatly into a social or solitary pattern. Instead, they drift — not because they're unstable, but because they're adapting. The structure of the behavior may change, but the emotional function stays the same: to regulate, to restore, to survive.

This drift is not inconsistency. It is pattern maintenance. When the ritual's purpose is to preserve coherence, any threat to that coherence — whether social tension or internal disruption — will be managed through a shift in behavior. What looks like escalation or avoidance from the outside is, internally, a precise recalibration: a response to emotional volatility the person doesn't yet know how to hold directly.

Take, for example, the social drinker. In the early stages, their ritual is embedded in a script: happy hours, friend groups, birthday parties. The behavior is camouflaged by connection. It feels communal, playful, even celebrated. But when something disrupts that script — a peer comments too candidly, a buried emotion rises too quickly, a sense of shame creeps in — the social ritual is no longer safe.

And so, the person shifts.

For a while, they drink alone. Not because they suddenly prefer solitude, but because the social space has been contaminated by confrontation — by something too close to the truth. Solitary use becomes a way to protect the ritual from challenge. It feels safer, quieter, more controllable. It returns the person to a state where they don't have to answer for their pain.

But the solitary mode has its own gravity. Without distraction or buffer, the emotions begin to swell. Rumination deepens. Shame thickens. The silence, once comforting, begins to echo. And so the person begins to reach again — not for healing, but for rhythm. They seek a new bar, a different crowd, a place where the ritual can resume without memory of the rupture.

This oscillation is not random. It's not a lack of willpower. It's a deeply intelligent adaptation to emotional threat. The person is protecting their last or only working strategy for coherence. When connection feels unsafe, they retreat. When the silence becomes unbearable, they return. The behavior is not broken — it is alive, reactive, self-regulating.

But this switching comes at a cost.

Each time they move between modes, something in their identity shifts. The person who performs joy at brunch becomes the one who cries into the sink at night. The one who isolates for weeks becomes the life of the party for a weekend. And the dissonance grows louder.

The person begins to split. The social self judges the solitary one. The solitary self resents the social mask. Each mode claims legitimacy — and yet neither can fully contain the truth.

This is the hidden exhaustion of addiction. Not just the behavior itself, but the emotional labor of constantly managing who you are allowed to be in which space. The person isn't just maintaining a ritual. They're maintaining an identity. One that is always at risk of being undone by honesty.

And still, they drift.
Not because they are lost.
But because the anchors keep breaking beneath them.

Pause and Consider

Where do you find yourself in this pattern?

Do you feel more like the one who performs? Or the one who hides?
Do you switch between the two?

What spaces feel safe enough for honesty — and which ones feel like they require the mask?

When you shift your behavior — from social to solitary, from outgoing to withdrawn — is it really a change in desire?
Or is it a change in what feels emotionally manageable?

Notice what happens when the ritual is challenged.
Who do you become?
What do you protect?

This isn't inconsistency. This is pattern preservation.

You were never failing by drifting.
You were responding — to threat, to loss, to the need for safety.

And even now, that response is trying to tell you something.

Not about who you are — but about what you've needed to survive.

Part II - Collapse

Eventually, the pattern breaks.

Not always with drama. Sometimes it happens in silence.
A missed cue. A shift in rhythm. A ritual that no longer
works the way it used to. You reach for the same relief,
follow the same steps — and this time, nothing lands. The
spiral continues, but the coherence is gone. The meaning
is gone. And what's left is the grief.

This is collapse.

Not because the person is weak. But because the structure
they were using to survive has outlived its usefulness. And
that loss — even when it comes in the form of addiction
— still hurts.

In this part, we don't offer solutions. We offer language.
We explore the weight of performing normalcy. The slow
hardening of identity. The rituals that look like connection
but are really just synchronized loneliness. And we look at
what happens when those patterns start to fracture —
when the addiction doesn't numb, doesn't connect,
doesn't save you anymore.

Collapse isn't the end.
It's the first honest moment.

And the only way forward is through it — not with shame,
but with clarity. Not with blame, but with grief. Because
what's breaking isn't just the habit. It's the entire story you
told yourself about what kept you safe.

And that story deserves to be honored — even as you let
it go.

Chapter 4 - When the Ritual Fails

Addiction doesn't end with a decision.
It ends with a flicker — a moment when the ritual stops giving back.

At first, it's subtle. The drink doesn't land quite right. The show doesn't calm you. The scroll doesn't soothe the ache in your chest. But you keep doing it anyway, because that's what's always worked. You tell yourself it was just a bad day. Just a dip. You'll try again tomorrow.

But tomorrow comes. And the return still doesn't.

This is where the collapse begins — not in some dramatic breakdown, but in the quiet realization that the thing you built your stability on can no longer hold your weight.

The behavior continues, but the meaning is gone.
The ritual remains, but the relief has vanished.
And without it, something inside starts to shake.

This chapter isn't about stopping.
It's about what happens when stopping starts to feel inevitable — not because you want to, but because the ritual no longer works.
And when the thing that once made you feel okay becomes the thing that reminds you just how lost you really are.

This is the beginning of the spiral — not because you're weak, but because you're grieving the last working piece of yourself.
And no one ever taught you how to fall with grace.

4.1

The Empty Ritual

There comes a point when the ritual stops working — but continues anyway.

It doesn't soothe. It doesn't center. It doesn't even distract. But it's still there. The same gestures. The same time of day. The same motions, now hollowed out. Like tracing the outline of a door that no longer leads anywhere.

This is the phase no one talks about — because it doesn't look dramatic. It doesn't come with sirens or consequences. On the outside, the behavior might look exactly the same. But on the inside, something has shifted. The spark is gone. The logic has cracked. The pattern that once made the person feel whole now leaves them more fractured than before.

And still, they do it.

Because stopping isn't as simple as realizing the ritual doesn't work. That moment — the awareness — is just the beginning. When the return disappears, the behavior becomes mechanical. Performed by muscle memory, not desire. It becomes an obligation, a superstition, a last-ditch attempt to feel something other than the dull ache of emptiness.

This is where the person begins to feel betrayed. Not by others. By the ritual.
By the thing that used to work.
By the structure they built to survive.

There's a specific kind of grief in this moment — not loud, not explosive. Just a quiet erosion. The person may not even realize they're grieving. They may think they're just tired, just irritable, just going through a rough patch. But beneath the surface, something is unraveling. Not because the ritual stopped working. But because they no longer know who they are without it.

The behavior continues not because it feels good, but because it's the only thing left.
And even that knowledge — that clarity — doesn't bring relief.

It brings shame.
Confusion.
And a question they can't quite name:
If this doesn't work anymore… what do I do now?

This is not recovery.
It's not surrender.
It's something else — something raw, something still breaking.
It's the body going through the motions of safety, even after the meaning has gone.

And it is unbearably human.

Vignette: After School

She started drinking around 10 a.m.
Not much. Just enough to take the edge off. Just enough
to quiet the part of her that still remembered she used to
want more.

By noon, the dishwasher was running, the laundry was
folded, and her glass had been refilled twice. She told
herself it was fine — this was her time. The only sliver of
the day that belonged to her. She was efficient. She had
routines. She kept the house standing.

By 2:45, the quiet broke.

The bus would be there soon. She felt her body tense at
the thought — not because she didn't love them. She did.
Of course she did. But the moment they walked in,
everything shifted. The noise, the needs, the unrelenting
cascade of "mom-mom-mom." It was like being touched
and needed and judged and ignored all at once.

By 3:15, the ritual began again. Smile. Snacks. Homework.
Pretend not to notice that one of them didn't say hi. She
topped off her glass at 4, standing at the sink, staring
through the window like it might give her a different
version of her life.

Dinner came. Then dishes. Then her partner — walking in
with that worn-out softness, like someone trying to be
useful without being in the way. They kissed her cheek and
asked how the day went. She shrugged. They smiled like
they always did, like they hoped the smile might bring her
back.

They took over bedtime. She told herself she was grateful. She *was* grateful. But the gratitude felt heavy — like a performance she was supposed to deliver. Like one more thing she couldn't get right.

She heard them reading to the kids, laughing softly, brushing hair back from little foreheads — and she hated how much she wanted to feel what they were clearly feeling. Connected. Present. Whole.

But all she could feel was the glass in her hand, the burn in her chest, and the slow, sinking certainty that she wasn't coming back. Not tonight. Maybe not tomorrow.

She could feel them watching her sometimes — hoping. Waiting.

And she hated that too.

At 9:30, her partner said something light. A joke about how good she looked today. A wink about maybe heading to bed early, together.

And something in her snapped.

She didn't scream. She didn't even raise her voice. She just cut the air between them with something sharp enough to draw blood — words she hadn't planned, words she barely meant, but words that got the job done.

Her partner stared for a moment, wounded but not surprised. They made a joke about it. Something self-deprecating. She said something sharp. They didn't respond.

She stayed at the sink. Alone. Again.
Her glass was still half full. She drank the rest and poured another.

She told herself she deserved it.
She told herself she was just tired.
She told herself that tomorrow would be better. That tomorrow she'd feel different. Want different. Be different.

And she stood there, glass in hand, quietly bracing herself for another day she hadn't asked for — grieving a self she could no longer name.

Vignette: After Dinner

He woke up early, as always.
Made the coffee. Made the lunches. Made sure the kids
had their shoes, their bags, their homework. He kissed his
wife's forehead while she blinked slowly at the ceiling,
whispering something about needing more sleep. He
didn't press her. He never did anymore.

By 8:30, the kids were gone, and he was already logged
into work. Meetings. Deadlines. Performance reviews. He
was good at his job — maybe too good. People relied on
him, asked for him by name. He turned down lunch plans
with colleagues because he needed to get home early.
Family came first. That's what he always said.

On the drive home, he let the quiet settle over him like
armor. He'd stopped listening to music in the car.
Sometimes the noise felt heavier than the silence. He
scrolled for a bit in the driveway before going inside —
just long enough to feel invisible. Just long enough to feel
like he didn't have to be needed.

He stepped through the door, kissed her again, made a
joke about dinner smelling amazing even though it didn't.
She nodded, didn't look up. He set the table. He got the
kids washed. He asked about school. He helped clean the
dishes. He helped with bedtime.

At 9:30, the house was still. He tried to initiate something
— not aggressively, just a soft brush of her back, a look, a
gesture. She flinched. Not physically, not obviously. Just
enough to remind him what the answer would be.

He made a joke about it. Something self-deprecating. She said something sharp. He didn't respond.

He went upstairs alone. Laid on the bed and opened his phone.
Scrolled reels. Scrolled news. Scrolled women he'd never meet smiling like they'd never be disappointed. Scrolled until the screen blurred and the clock said 1:13 a.m.

He didn't cry. He didn't even feel angry. He just felt... forgotten.
Not by her.
By the story of himself he was trying so hard to keep alive.

He wanted to be wanted.
He wanted to be seen.
But more than anything, he wanted to believe that all the things he was doing still meant something.

Downstairs, she poured another glass.
Upstairs, he kept scrolling.
Waiting for her to come to bed.
Still thinking, somehow, maybe this night would be different.

Pause and Consider

Breathe.

Right now, if your chest feels tight or your eyes are stinging or your body has gone a little still — that's not weakness. That's recognition. And recognition is one of the hardest things we can do.

If something in that story felt familiar, please know this: You are not broken.

You are not failing.

You are not alone.

This story is far more common than it should be — not because people are weak, but because we live in a world that asks too much, gives too little, and rarely stops long enough to ask how any of us are actually doing.

The ritual isn't the problem. It was your solution. It was the system you built to survive the parts of your life that no one else was holding with you.

Maybe you've been doing it for so long, you don't know what's underneath. Maybe part of you doesn't want to find out. That's okay. You don't have to fix anything today.

Just ask yourself this, gently:

What is the ritual protecting me from?

You don't need the answer right away.

Just stay curious.

Just stay kind to yourself.

Just stay.

4.2

The Escalation Spiral

When the ritual stops working, most people don't stop. They escalate. It doesn't come from rebellion or recklessness — it comes from grief. A grief so quiet it's rarely named, but so powerful it demands action. The person increases the behavior not because they're chasing a high, but because they're chasing coherence. Relief. The return of something that once made life feel manageable.

At first, the shift is small. A second drink when one used to be enough. Another episode. Another mile. Another purchase. Just a little more — nothing serious. Nothing unexplainable. But the logic beneath the behavior has changed. They're no longer engaging the ritual to feel good. They're engaging it to avoid falling apart.

When the original dose doesn't work, the body tightens. The mind scrambles. And instead of questioning the ritual, the person questions themselves. *Maybe I didn't try hard enough. Maybe I didn't give it the right conditions. Maybe tomorrow.* So they try again. And again. Until the pattern begins to consume the spaces around it.

What used to be a quiet strategy becomes a constant preoccupation. When will I do it next? How can I do it without being noticed? What if someone finds out? What if I stop? What if I can't?

Escalation is not the start of the spiral. It is the spiral trying to fix itself.

And it's understandable. Because stopping the behavior doesn't just mean change — it means loss. It means confronting the fact that the system they trusted, depended on, built themselves around, is no longer working. And for many, that kind of honesty feels too dangerous to face directly. So instead, they work harder. They hide more. They build new justifications, new rhythms, new rules — all in service of preserving the ritual that once gave them meaning.

But eventually, even the escalation doesn't deliver. The relief becomes shorter. The shame gets louder. The structure begins to crack under its own weight. And the person is left doing something that no longer helps, no longer heals, but still feels impossible to let go of.

This is the moment when addiction no longer looks like indulgence.
It looks like survival.
It looks like someone trying to outrun a collapse they can already feel beneath their feet.

Vignette: The Breaking Point

It started with the laundry.

He had folded it and left it on the bed, like he always did, neat stacks organized by drawer. She walked in, wine glass half full, and stared at it like it was a threat. He asked her something soft — something stupid, really. "Rough day?" Maybe he smiled too much. Maybe not enough. She didn't answer.

Instead, she walked past the laundry, kicked off her shoes, and disappeared into the bathroom without closing the door. He waited. Gave her time. Gave her space. That's what he did.

When she came out, he tried again. "I'm worried about you." He meant it.

She shrugged. "I'm fine."

"You're not," he said. It wasn't an accusation. It was a fracture.

She stood still. Her body didn't flinch, but her mouth tightened. "I get shit done. The kids are fine. The house is fine."

"I didn't say it wasn't," he replied. "But I don't know who you are anymore."

And that's when it broke.

She turned on him — not shouting, but sharp, clipped, surgical. "You want me to fall into your arms after I've been touched and talked at and needed all fucking day? You think folding the laundry makes you my savior? You think helping with bedtime earns you sex?"

He opened his mouth to speak, but she kept going. "You're not helping me. You're *witnessing* me drown and calling it devotion."

He froze. Not because she was wrong — but because she wasn't.

He wanted to say something. Anything. To reach across the space between them. But he'd spent so long performing usefulness, he no longer knew how to be present. He had learned to offer tasks in place of love. She had learned to drink instead of ask for help.

He looked down. "I don't know what to do anymore."

"Neither do I," she whispered. And for the first time in a long time, her voice cracked.

He stepped forward, hand half-raised motioning for a hug, but she turned away before he could reach her. Not out of anger. Out of fear that if he touched her, she might actually feel something. And it would be too much.

He stood there in silence, surrounded by folded clothes no one would put away.
She went downstairs.
He went to bed.
Neither of them picked up the pieces.

"You were never meant to earn your own worth. The collapse is just where the pretending ends."

4.3

The Unnamed Grief

When the ritual fails, we don't just lose a behavior — we lose a system. A rhythm. A story that once gave shape to our days and meaning to our pain. And while the world may focus on the damage caused by addiction, what's rarely acknowledged is the grief that follows its collapse.

It's not just about stopping. It's about losing the last part of your life that felt predictable. Even if it was hurting you. Even if it was hollow. It was still *yours*. You knew what to expect from it. You knew how to move through it. You knew who you were inside it.

When that's gone, what's left is not relief.
It's confusion. Disorientation. Silence.

This grief doesn't come in tears. It doesn't always come with words. It shows up as restlessness. As shame. As numbness that won't lift no matter how many hours of sleep or sober days go by. It shows up as the sudden urge to return to the ritual — not because you want the high, but because you miss the structure. The meaning. The shape it gave your life.

This grief is hard to name because no one told you that addiction was doing something *for* you. That it was holding something your body didn't know how to carry alone. And now, without it, you're not just hurting. You're raw. Unprotected. Unstructured. And utterly exposed to the very emotions the ritual once contained.

You may find yourself angry. Not just at the behavior — but at the world. At the people who never showed up. At the childhood you had to navigate without a guide. At the emptiness that no one warned you about. That anger is valid. It's not a setback. It's part of the mourning.

You are not grieving the loss of a vice.
You are grieving the collapse of your coherence.

And that grief is holy. It means you're finally telling the truth. It means the silence is no longer enough. It means you're beginning to feel what the pattern once protected you from. Which also means, for the first time in a long time...

You might be ready to be held.
Not by a behavior.
But by something real.

Vignette: The Last Twenty

He counted the cash three times.

Crinkled bills, a handful of coins, and a hollow kind of hope. It wasn't enough. Not for what he needed. Not anymore.

There was a time when a little did the trick. A sip, a pill, a line. One hit and the world would tilt just enough to soften. Just enough to quiet the noise and bring him back into his own skin. But that was a long time ago.

Now it took more… a lot more. And he didn't have it.

He sat on the edge of the bed, head in hands, trying to decide whether to pace or pray. Neither sounded helpful. He opened his phone, closed it again. The notifications meant nothing. No one was coming. No one was watching.

The ache in his chest wasn't panic. It was something deeper — something colder. The kind of hollow that creeps in when the ritual breaks and nothing rushes in to replace it. His hands trembled, not from withdrawal exactly, but from absence. From the sudden realization that *this is it*. This is what it feels like when the thing you've built your whole rhythm around stops giving anything back.

He leaned against the wall and let the stillness crawl in. For a second, he thought he might cry. But nothing came. Just that soft, scraping grief that doesn't announce itself. That just… *settles*.

He thought about calling someone. But what would he say? "It doesn't work anymore"? "I don't know who I am without this"? He didn't want to be comforted. He didn't want to be judged. He just wanted to not feel this — this sharp, unfixable clarity.

For a flicker of a moment, he saw it clearly: the chase hadn't made him whole. It had made him empty — the ritual a hallway that led nowhere. The high he kept reaching for wasn't relief. It was a delay. A postponement of pain he was now meeting, face to face.

And it was unbearable.

But it was also real.

He exhaled. Not in surrender, not in peace.
Just to prove to himself that he still could.

Then he saw the last twenty he needed on the floor crinkled up next to an empty pack of booze, out of instinct he sprinted to it.

He reached for his phone, texted his dealer, and left.

Pause and Consider

Not every addiction ends in a sprint toward a dealer.

Some end in a text you promised you'd never send.

Some end in a refrigerator door you don't remember opening.

Some end in a browser tab. A lie. A day you swore would be different.

Relapse is not reserved for the most visible addictions. It shows up in any pattern we built to survive — any ritual we trusted to hold what no one else could.

So if you're asking yourself:

Why do I always go back to him?

Why can't I just stop eating?

Why do I keep doing this thing that I know doesn't help?

The answer is:

Because the pattern once worked.

Because your body remembers the relief, even when your mind doesn't want it.

Because repetition feels safer than emptiness — even when it hurts.

This isn't a flaw in your character.

It's a reflection of your need.

And every time you see it clearly — even if you still go back — you're closer to building something new.

Not because you finally deserve healing.

But because you never stopped deserving it in the first place.

Chapter 5 - Becoming the Performance

Not everyone falls apart in the way we expect.

Some people don't scream, or run, or get caught. They don't spiral in public. They don't make headlines or cry in stairwells. They get quieter. Sharper. They hold the world together with calendar invites and polite smiles and routines that no longer mean anything. They stop reaching out — not because they're okay, but because reaching out would require telling the truth. And the truth no longer feels like it has a place.

This is the performance collapse — the slow, quiet transformation of identity into something that can survive visibility. It doesn't look like despair. It looks like competence. It looks like "still showing up." It looks like someone who hasn't missed a deadline, hasn't broken down, hasn't let anyone in.

After the ritual fails, and the spiral has burned through whatever relief was left, what often remains is structure. Performance. The self becomes a task list. And the person begins to live like an actor who never takes off the costume — because they've forgotten who they were before the script.

It's not inauthentic. It's not fake. It's *what's left*.

This chapter is about that performance. About the masks we stop realizing we're wearing. About the quiet dignity of those who "hold it together" so well they start to disappear inside the image. It's not a chapter about lying. It's a chapter about survival. And about the cost of coherence built entirely on being okay.

5.1

Identity as Armor

There's a moment in collapse when everything sharpens. Not in chaos, but in control. The person who once spiraled outward begins to spiral inward. They grow quieter, more efficient. They wake up early, stay late, respond to every message, hit every deadline. They stop arguing, stop reacting, stop reaching out. They become consistent. Polite. Impressive, even.

And to the outside world, it looks like they've recovered.

But they haven't. They've just learned how to carry it without letting it spill.

This is the stage when addiction — or any pattern built to hold pain — loses its external form and becomes an identity. When the ritual no longer offers relief, the person becomes the relief. The self hardens into a role, and the role becomes a shield. Not just from others, but from themselves. Because to stop performing would mean facing the truth: that the pain never left. It just got quieter.

They no longer do the behavior. They *are* the identity. The drinker becomes dependable. The codependent becomes strong. The overachiever becomes successful. The one who couldn't stop becomes the one who never breaks. And behind that image is silence — not peace, not resolution, just the kind of silence that settles in when the volume has been turned down on your inner world for too long.

There is a deep kind of grief in this kind of strength. It isn't chosen. It's inherited from years of having no better option. People celebrate this version of you. They admire your grit, your patience, your work ethic. They never notice that your laugh doesn't reach your eyes anymore. They stop asking if you're okay because you've become so good at not needing to be.

This isn't deceit. It's design. The body and mind reorganize around survival. You become a person who works, shows up, meets expectations. You stop expecting things in return. You stop waiting for someone to see through it. Because it's easier to be admired than to risk being seen.

And so the armor stays on.

Not because it makes you stronger.
But because taking it off would mean remembering who you were before you needed it.

5.2

The Dignity of Holding It Together

Some people never fall apart in public. They go to work. They show up for their families. They pay the bills, answer texts, organize playdates, manage calendars. Their homes are clean. Their sentences are coherent. Their smiles arrive on cue.

These are the people who know how to survive collapse without drawing attention to it. Not because they're stronger than others — but because they had to learn how to keep going long before anyone ever asked how they were doing. Their strength didn't grow in peace. It grew in silence.

There is a quiet kind of dignity in this way of surviving. It's not dramatic. It's not romantic. It's simply a choice — one made over and over again, often without thinking — to stay upright in a world that never offered to hold them.

These are the people who carry the weight without showing the strain. Not because they want to be invisible, but because they've come to believe that breaking down would make them a burden. And being a burden, to them, would be worse than being in pain.

They learn to manage themselves meticulously. Routines become sacred. Efficiency becomes identity. They say things like "I'm just tired" or "I've got it" or "Don't worry about me." And often, no one does. Because when someone looks like they're holding it together, the world stops asking if they need help.

What most people don't see is how much effort that holding takes. The sleep-deprived nights. The silent self-negotiations. The moments of nearly asking for help before smiling instead. They don't see the cost of staying composed in every room. They don't see the private moments — at the sink, in the car, at the end of another too-long day — when the mask stays on not because it's comfortable, but because there's no safe place to set it down.

And yet, despite all of it, there is honor in this kind of strength. Not because it's ideal — but because it's real. Because it's the best some people can do with what they've been given. Because it speaks to an inner architecture so resilient it held together even after the ritual failed.

But dignity doesn't mean sustainability.
There's only so long you can hold yourself together before the effort begins to eat you from the inside.

And eventually, even the most beautifully constructed self starts to show cracks.

Vignette: Gold Star

They called her unstoppable.

She had three kids, a full-time job, aging parents to care for, and still found time to volunteer at the school book fair. She baked gluten-free cupcakes because one of the kids in her son's class had celiac. She color-coded her Google Calendar. She remembered birthdays. She donated to fundraisers. She replied to emails before anyone else even opened them.

At work, her manager said she was a "dream to have on the team." At home, her friends called her "Superwoman." She laughed every time, a little too hard, like she didn't mind. Like she believed it.

She kept a candle lit at her desk, lemon-scented. Wore clean sneakers. Texted back with perfect punctuation. People wanted to be like her. People thought she had it together.

What they didn't see was how every compliment about her strength made her feel more alone.

Because strength, to her, wasn't empowerment. It was obligation. It was performance. It was the armor she built because she knew no one was coming. And now, she couldn't set it down without feeling like she'd be dropping the very thing that made her worth keeping.

Most days, she functioned fine. Beautifully, even. But there were days — days like this one — when she got in the car, pulled out of the parking lot, and found herself fantasizing, just for a second, about turning into oncoming traffic.

Not out of rage. Not even out of despair.
Just… relief.

The idea that everything would stop. That no one would need anything from her. That she wouldn't have to explain herself, or disappoint anyone, or spend another night pretending the glass of wine she poured was about taste and not survival.

She always kept driving.

She turned on music. Rolled down the window. Adjusted the temperature. Smiled at the crossing guard. No one knew. They never would.

Because the world doesn't stop for the strong.
It leans on them.
And she knew that if she broke, it wouldn't be called pain.
It would be called selfish.

So she drove home.
Picked up dinner.
Smiled through bath time.
And folded laundry while her heart quietly screamed for an exit she no longer believed she deserved.

Stop and Consider

If you've ever had that thought — even fleeting — about swerving into traffic, disappearing, or not waking up...

You are not broken.
You are not dramatic.
You are carrying too much alone.

Please don't keep doing that.

There are people who *do* want to help carry it — and you don't have to explain everything to deserve that help.

Call or text **988** (U.S. Suicide & Crisis Lifeline) — it's free, confidential, and available 24/7.

If you're outside the U.S., visit findahelpline.com for international support options.

You don't have to be at your worst to reach out.
You just have to be tired of pretending you're fine.

"*I think the saddest people always try their hardest to make people happy. Because they know what it feels like to feel absolutely worthless, and they don't want anyone else to feel like that.*"
— Robin Williams

5.3

The Resignation

At some point, the performance stops feeling like a role
and starts feeling like reality. You forget when you stopped
reaching for connection and started accepting that you
were only safe when you were useful. It doesn't happen all
at once. There's no dramatic moment. Just the slow, quiet
accumulation of unmet needs, dismissed feelings, and
unanswered longings that harden into something that
looks a lot like strength from the outside.

You're not faking it anymore. You're living it. You get up,
get dressed, answer emails, show up for other people. You
know the right things to say and when to say them. You've
learned how to be just vulnerable enough to seem
authentic, just put together enough to avoid questions. No
one checks in anymore, and if they do, they ask about your
productivity — not your pain. And that makes sense,
because you've trained them to believe you're fine.
Sometimes, you almost believe it yourself.

But underneath the calm, a deeper truth hums: you've
stopped hoping. Not in a dramatic, world-ending kind of
way. You just stopped believing that things might feel
different. The mask isn't something you wear — it's
something you grew into. The lines between performance
and personhood blurred until you no longer remember
what it felt like to be loved without having to earn it.

That's what resignation looks like. Not collapse, but
emotional hibernation. You're still functioning, still
present, still doing the things that people point to as signs
that you're okay. But the inner world has gone still. Muted.
You've made peace with being alone in your pain, not

because you want to be, but because somewhere along the way, it started to feel like the only safe option.

You resign yourself to being strong, not because you're fearless, but because you're terrified that if you stopped being the strong one, no one would know how to hold you. You stop asking to be seen. You stop trusting that being seen is safe. And the more others praise your composure, the more isolated you become — held up as a model of resilience, when in truth, you're surviving by disappearing inside your role.

And still, somewhere deep beneath the layers of routine and restraint, the part of you that aches to be known is still alive. It hasn't given up. It's just waiting — for permission, for safety, for someone to say, "You don't have to hold this alone anymore." That part of you remembers what it felt like to be whole. And it's still hoping, even now, that one day, you'll come back.

5.4

When the Armor Cracks

Resignation is not the end of the spiral. It's a narrowing. A moment where identity fuses with endurance. You're no longer just surviving — you're surviving as someone who doesn't need help, doesn't make mistakes, doesn't fall apart. But eventually, the performance breaks. Not all at once. Just a slip. A sigh. A moment when the mask wobbles.

When the armor cracks, it doesn't always mean collapse. Sometimes it means *reach*. The person, desperate for a sense of belonging, starts looking outward again — not necessarily for support, but for affirmation. And the most accessible form of affirmation often comes from others who share the pattern.

This is where community can become camouflage. The group that drinks the same way, shops the same way, scrolls the same way, works out the same way — suddenly becomes a mirror. Not of recovery, but of justification. "See? I'm not the only one." "It's not that bad." "Everyone I know does this."

The ritual adapts. It stops being solitary. It becomes social. The behavior doesn't go away — it becomes synchronized. And the person begins to mistake *relatability* for *relief*.

They might start sharing memes about "wine o'clock," joking about doomscrolling until 3 a.m., laughing about being "addicted to the gym." It looks like connection, but it's actually insulation. A way to reinforce the behavior without having to call it a problem. Because if others are doing it too — and still functioning — then maybe this isn't addiction. Maybe this is just life.

But beneath that logic is still the grief. Still the exhaustion. Still the fear of being exposed. The person hasn't escaped the spiral — they've just found a way to blend it into the background of their social life. The addiction gets quieter, more socially acceptable, more disguised — but no less damaging.

This is the final stage of performance: when the ritual is no longer hidden, but normalized. When the world affirms the behavior enough that the person stops questioning it themselves. It's not that they feel better. It's that they stop expecting to feel anything else.

And still, the part of them that remembers what it felt like to be whole hasn't left.

It's just been waiting — under the armor, beneath the smile, behind the laughter —

for a moment when community could mean *healing* instead of *hiding*.

Chapter 6 - Community in Disguise

Addiction doesn't always isolate people. Sometimes, it brings them together.

We imagine addiction as a solitary thing — a person alone in a room, repeating a ritual no one else sees. But that's not the only way it lives. Sometimes, addiction happens in groups. In brunch tables, in online communities, in gyms, in bars, in relationships, in workplaces where overwork is a badge of honor. It happens in silence — but also in chorus.

There's a kind of intimacy in shared spirals. A language. A rhythm. Everyone drinking at the same pace. Everyone laughing at the same kind of numbness. Everyone pretending the joke is louder than the ache. It feels like belonging — but it's not. It's *synchronization*. People moving in parallel, not together. Each person privately hoping that the presence of others means they're okay.

But being seen is not the same as being held. And being mirrored is not the same as being met.

This chapter is about that confusion — about the difference between community and cover. It's about the people we spiral with, the rituals we preserve through each other, and the illusion of intimacy that forms when everyone is just trying to keep their own pain from spilling over.

Here, we'll name how community can become camouflage.
How "support" can become silence.
How blame can become a substitute for grief.
And how healing might require not more people — but different kinds of presence.

Because when addiction becomes social, it doesn't disappear.

It just learns how to blend in.

6.1

Lonely Together

Western culture doesn't talk about loneliness directly. It reframes it — as independence, ambition, strength. We celebrate the solo grind, the late nights, the high-functioning breakdowns. We admire people who suffer quietly and keep showing up. The narrative isn't "are you okay?" It's "how do you do it all?"

In this context, addiction doesn't look like a warning sign. It looks like bonding.

It looks like happy hour with coworkers after a brutal week — everyone drinking too fast, too much, laughing a little too loudly, already half-regretting tomorrow. It looks like the parent group text full of memes about being "wine moms" or "coffee zombies," each message another notch in the collective spiral. It looks like the partner who joins you in a binge because "we've both had a hard day." It looks like 2 a.m. gaming sessions where no one talks about why they don't want to log off.

It looks like connection. But it's not. It's choreography.

Each person performing closeness while carefully avoiding anything that might disrupt the illusion. The ritual becomes the relationship. You keep showing up because they're showing up — and maybe that's enough. Maybe it has to be. Because talking about the ache underneath would break the spell.

This isn't a coincidence. It's cultural design. In many Western contexts, community has been flattened into proximity. Being physically near others — in a workspace, in a group chat, in a relationship — is mistaken for emotional safety. But emotional safety requires presence, witnessing, vulnerability. And most people in these environments were never taught how to offer that — or even ask for it.

So we become lonely together. Functionally adjacent. Performing intimacy through shared behavior instead of honest connection. Addiction thrives in this environment because it gives the body what the culture refuses to provide: rhythm, regulation, relief. The ritual steps in where the community structure should have been. And the more socially acceptable the addiction, the harder it is to name what's actually happening.

When everyone's numbing the same way, no one looks like they're in pain.
When everyone's smiling, no one asks who's still grieving.

And when addiction is mirrored in others, it becomes easier to pretend it's not a problem — just a lifestyle. Just a preference. Just a phase. But deep down, the body knows. The body always knows.

It knows when the laughter is forced.
It knows when the group energy feels thin.
It knows when you leave the party lonelier than when you arrived.

And it knows when your rituals have become the only thing keeping you from realizing how alone you've felt for years — even in rooms full of people who say they love you.

Western culture didn't invent loneliness — but it may be the first to commodify it so effectively. Our rituals of connection are often just rituals of distraction. Shopping. Streaming. Substances. Clicks. Everything is available. Everything is immediate. And everything is just far enough away from intimacy to feel safe.

In *Brave New World*, Aldous Huxley imagined a society that didn't repress its citizens with fear — but with comfort. With "soma," a drug that kept people docile, untroubled, agreeable. No pain, no grief, no deep questions. Just pleasure, routine, and distraction. It wasn't a dystopia of violence. It was a dystopia of numbness.

That world was fiction. Ours is just branded better.

Modern society doesn't hand out soma. It offers its own versions: alcohol marketed as empowerment, overwork praised as ambition, constant digital connection mistaken for closeness. Pain isn't confronted — it's optimized, filtered, or scrolled past. And when the soul finally screams for meaning, the culture offers another product, another program, another coping strategy that promises relief without ever asking you to feel.

Addiction thrives here. Not because people are weak, but because they are responding *perfectly* to a system that has made emotional suppression not just acceptable — but aspirational.

And when everyone's numbing together, no one is asked to heal.

Just to keep going.
Just to fit in.
Just to perform their role in the illusion of intimacy.

Lonely together.

Exactly as designed.

Pause and Consider

Are you uncomfortable right now?
Good.
That discomfort might be the most honest thing you've
felt all day.

Ask yourself — where is it coming from?
Is it guilt? Fear? Resistance? Fatigue?
Or maybe it's something older, something quieter: the
sense that the life you've been performing doesn't quite fit
who you are anymore.

Now ask:
What are my values?
Where did I learn them?
Who benefits from me believing those things?

When was the last time you chose a behavior — a
moment, a conversation, a response — with real intention
rather than as an escape?
When was the last time your rituals felt like acts of
meaning, not just *ways to pass the time?*

Discomfort is not the enemy.
It's the doorway.
And it only opens if you stay long enough to knock.

6.2

The Need to Blame

When the pain gets too close to the surface, someone has to be responsible for it. That's how blame works — not as a conscious strategy, but as an emotional reflex. It gives shape to discomfort. It organizes chaos. It offers a storyline where there was only ache.

Blame doesn't just arise from trauma or betrayal. It also emerges from ambiguity — from the slow, unbearable question: *Why do I still feel like this?* And Western society, ever eager to sell answers, is more than happy to step in.

Blame becomes a product. A performance. A guided emotional transaction.

You don't need to explore your patterns — you just need a villain. And the culture has plenty to offer: blame your ex, your mother, your hormones, your boss, your phone, your metabolism. Blame your schedule. Blame your zodiac sign. Blame your trauma — but only in bite-sized, monetizable ways. You can even buy merchandise to prove it: wine glasses that say "Because kids," candles labeled "man tears," T-shirts that read "overstimulated and underappreciated." Pain becomes branding. Grief becomes lifestyle.

And in a world that packages suffering as content, taking responsibility for your part in the pattern feels almost subversive. Healing isn't nearly as marketable as cathartic rage. Blame sells. Grief requires silence. Grief requires slowing down — and slowing down doesn't generate clicks, sales, or algorithms that affirm your worldview.

So instead, you're handed narratives that keep the fire burning. You scroll through curated anger, nodding along to posts that affirm your resentments. You find yourself in echo chambers that feed the fantasy of accountability without asking anything of you. And slowly, without realizing it, your pain becomes public — but never personal. It's outsourced. It's aestheticized. It's rehearsed so many times that you forget what the original wound even was.

The danger isn't just that you're blaming someone else. It's that blame becomes the structure you live inside. It gives you something to push against. Something to define yourself by. It offers just enough coherence to keep you from unraveling — but never enough clarity to truly let go.

And the longer you stay in that structure, the more difficult it becomes to grieve. Because grief would require collapsing the narrative. It would require saying: *They hurt me, yes — but I've also stayed in this pattern. I've also contributed to it. I've also avoided myself inside it.* That kind of truth doesn't trend. That kind of truth doesn't win arguments.

But it heals.

Because blame might feel powerful, but it's brittle. It cannot hold you through collapse. It cannot anchor you through grief. It cannot offer you the intimacy you've been longing for. It can only delay the moment when you finally turn inward and say: *What am I still carrying? And what am I ready to release?*

In a society that teaches you how to blame and who to blame — choosing grief is revolutionary.

It means reclaiming your story.
It means refusing to perform pain for approval.
It means being brave enough to feel the part no one else can fix for you.

Vignette: It Was Easier When It Was His Fault

She slammed the cabinet harder than she meant to. The sound echoed through the kitchen, sharp and theatrical, like punctuation for a sentence she hadn't said out loud.

He was late. Again. Not by much — maybe fifteen minutes — but enough. Enough to tip the evening into resentment. Enough to remind her that he always did this. Enough to build a case.

When he walked in, she didn't look up. Didn't say hello. He set his keys down quietly, sensing the temperature.

"Sorry," he offered. "Traffic — "

"Sure," she cut in, flat. "It always is."

They moved around each other like strangers pretending to know the choreography. She wiped the counters with more force than necessary. He busied himself with the mail. She waited for him to ask how her day was, and when he didn't, she told herself it was proof. Proof that she was alone. Proof that he didn't care. Proof that she was right.

Because being right felt safer than being sad.

When they finally sat down to eat, the silence thickened. He tried to make conversation. She shut it down. He asked if she was okay. She shrugged. He apologized again. She told him not to bother.

And inside, she hoped he would fight her. She hoped he would push back, lose his temper, say something awful — something she could use to justify the aching distance that had been building for months. But he didn't. He just looked tired. Not dismissive. Not cruel. Just tired.

That made her angrier.

After dinner, he disappeared upstairs. She stayed behind to clear the dishes, her chest tight with unshed emotion. She wanted to cry but didn't. She wanted to scream but didn't. Instead, she stood at the sink, staring into the soapy water, replaying the argument that never happened.

And then, without ceremony, the story cracked.

Not loudly. Not all at once. Just a quiet shift — a flicker of recognition.

This isn't about him being late.
This is about me being lonely.
And blaming him lets me stay angry instead of heartbroken.

The thought startled her. It didn't absolve him. It didn't erase the pattern. But it opened something. A space between the blame and the pain. A space where she could see herself — not just as the one who was hurt, but as someone who had learned to make her hurt into a weapon.

She leaned against the counter and let herself feel it — the grief she'd been avoiding with every sarcastic remark, every silent treatment, every imagined scorecard.

And for the first time in a long time, she didn't try to win. She just let herself ache.
Not because he failed her.
But because she was finally ready to stop failing herself.

6.3

Rituals That Pass for Love

Not all addictions are solitary. Some are shared — quietly, rhythmically, like a dance neither person remembers learning.

These rituals don't always look destructive. In fact, many are mistaken for connection. The couple that always drinks together. The friends who bond over workaholism. The parents who co-sign each other's emotional avoidance. The partners who binge shows night after night and call it quality time. From the outside, these relationships appear close. Intimate, even. But look closer, and you'll see that what's being preserved isn't closeness — it's distance.

In these spaces, love becomes fused with coping. You're not supporting each other — you're supporting the structure that helps you both avoid what you're not ready to face. You regulate each other's discomfort by reinforcing the pattern, not by witnessing the pain underneath. And the deeper the shared ritual becomes, the harder it is to tell where you end and the pattern begins.

This is especially dangerous in relationships where caretaking becomes the language of love. One person spirals, the other rescues. One breaks down, the other holds it together. The roles feel like devotion, but they are often just adaptations — a mutual agreement to maintain the system. Over time, the caretaking becomes its own form of addiction. Helping someone survive becomes the ritual. Feeling needed replaces feeling known.

And when that dynamic is interrupted — when one person starts to heal, or shifts the pattern — the rupture is immediate. The spiral no longer syncs. The regulation fails. And what's left is the painful realization that *the relationship was built on the pattern, not the person.*

Western culture only deepens this confusion. It tells us that love is about sacrifice, loyalty, holding on no matter what. It offers storylines where pain is proof of passion, where chaos is a kind of chemistry, where drama equals depth. It rarely shows us what real intimacy looks like: emotional accountability, mutual regulation, softness without a performance. And so we grow up thinking that rituals of avoidance are signs of commitment.

But love — real love — is not a shared script of survival. It's not staying up drinking together just to feel connected. It's not tolerating each other's addictions because confronting them might risk the relationship. Love is not the silent agreement to never name what hurts.

Love is not supposed to be what helps you stay hidden. It's supposed to be what helps you come home to yourself.

And if a ritual keeps you close but never seen, it might not be love.
It might just be familiarity dressed as safety.
It might be the pattern — not the person — you're holding on to.

6.4

Codependence as Addiction

Codependence is addiction.

Not metaphorically. Not poetically. Literally.

It is a behavioral, emotional, and psychological dependency — one that forms not around a substance, but around *control through caretaking*. It is a ritualized pattern of self-erasure, driven by the need to stabilize the emotions of others in order to avoid confronting your own. And like all addictions, it starts with relief. It begins with a payoff: praise, appreciation, identity, purpose.

But it becomes unsustainable. The pattern escalates. You give more. Ask for less. Shape-shift faster. Break your own boundaries quietly, rationally, even lovingly — until you begin to forget what they were in the first place.

And like any addiction, codependence is not random. It is a strategy. A survival mechanism rooted in a deep belief: *If I am useful, I am safe. If I am needed, I cannot be abandoned. If I can manage their chaos, I don't have to feel my own.*

It mirrors substance addiction in every structural way:

- There is compulsion: the urge to help, to fix, to absorb.

- There is withdrawal: the panic that arises when someone pulls away or doesn't need you.

- There is escalation: increasing levels of emotional labor to maintain connection.

- There is ritual: the repeated cycle of depleting yourself to soothe someone else — followed by temporary relief, followed by emptiness.

- And most crucially, there is denial: the belief that it's love, when it's actually a way to avoid your own vulnerability.

This is what most recovery models miss. They treat codependence as a personality trait, not a chemical loop. They address boundaries and patterns, but not cravings. They give language to the behaviors, but not to the withdrawal that follows when you stop performing usefulness. They don't name that the grief of letting go is not just relational — it is neurological. It is existential.

Because when your identity has been built around holding others, the absence of someone to hold can feel like death. And the temptation is always to relapse — not into substances, but into *service*. Into overfunctioning. Into emotional absorption. Into being the strong one again, because collapse feels shameful and stillness feels unsafe.

But codependence is not selflessness. It is survival masquerading as care.

And until we name it for what it is — an addiction to control through relational performance — we will keep romanticizing patterns that are quietly eroding the people who seem the most "put together."

Codependents are not weak.
They are some of the most disciplined addicts in the world.
And recovery will not begin until we stop calling it kindness and start calling it what it is: a cycle of emotional avoidance built on the fantasy that love can be earned, needs to be earned. Often without ever stopping to consider that if that were true, *"Why is no one trying to earn my love?"*

6.5

When Leaving Feels Like Betrayal

Recovery, when it finally begins, often comes with a cost no one prepares you for: you might have to leave people behind.

Not because you want to. Not because you're better than them. But because the patterns you once shared — the drinks, the jokes, the overwork, the caretaking, the silence — were never just habits. They were *contracts*. Agreements made in pain. Reinforced through ritual. And healing breaks the contract.

When you stop playing your part in someone else's spiral, you don't just free yourself — you disrupt the system. You stop absorbing, stop rescuing, stop numbing in sync. You become unpredictable. And in the fragile economy of shared addiction, unpredictability feels like betrayal.

They may not say it out loud. But you'll feel it. The cooling of the room. The jokes that land differently. The invitations that stop coming. The subtle — or not so subtle — punishment for changing the rhythm you used to share.

And it hurts.

Because leaving doesn't just mean walking away from dysfunction. It means walking away from the *only version of connection you've known* — even if that connection was never real intimacy. Even if it was never safe. It was still something. And in the absence of something, the silence can feel unbearable.

This is the part of recovery no one romanticizes: the loneliness that follows honesty. The grief of realizing that your growth costs you people. The aching awareness that the rituals you're shedding were not just coping mechanisms — they were social glue.

You may find yourself asking: *Why does getting better feel so lonely?*

The answer is simple, but not easy: because healing is honest, and most of what passed for connection was not.

The truth is, some people won't come with you.
Some friendships won't survive your boundaries.
Some relationships won't tolerate your clarity.
Some communities won't know what to do with your softness once you stop performing strength.

And that's not failure. That's fidelity — to yourself.

Leaving is not betrayal.
It's the beginning of belonging.
Not to a group, not to a pattern, but to the version of you that no longer needs to disappear to be loved.

6.6

Not Everyone Who Stays Is Safe

When you begin to heal, not everyone leaves. And at first, that feels like a gift. It feels like proof that your growth doesn't have to cost you everything. It feels like evidence that some people can handle your truth. But over time, if you look closely, you may begin to notice something quieter — and harder to admit.

Not everyone who stays is safe.

Some of the people who remain are not staying out of love. They're staying out of habit. Or obligation. Or because your old patterns were meeting their unspoken needs. They might applaud your strength while quietly resenting your boundaries. They might say they support your healing but subtly punish your clarity. They might still need you to be the emotional sponge — just with better language now. Their presence is not necessarily a reflection of growth. Sometimes, it's a reflection of how well you learned to perform.

This is one of the hardest parts of recovery — realizing that the people who benefitted from your self-abandonment may not be able to walk with you into self-repair. That the comfort of their presence doesn't mean it's safe to stay the same. And that love, without accountability, eventually becomes a weight. You may find yourself grieving relationships that never asked you to be whole, only to be helpful. You may find yourself aching for honesty in places where politeness now masks resentment. And you may realize that presence is not the same as partnership — especially when healing begins to rearrange what you're willing to carry.

But not all who stay are stuck.

Some people will surprise you.

They may not get it right at first. They may flinch. They may shut down. They may even react defensively when your growth reflects back their avoidance. But something in them shifts. They hear you. They stay curious. And slowly, something rare begins to happen — not just support, but mutual repair.

These are the people who begin to meet your accountability with their own.

They don't just say, "I'm glad you're doing better." They say, "I'm sorry I didn't ask more direct questions."
They don't just applaud your boundaries. They say, "I see now how I made you carry my feelings for me."
They don't just witness your grief. They say, "I treated your pain like an indictment. I didn't know how to hold it."

And then they say the thing you might have stopped believing you'd ever hear:

"We both deserved better. And I want to grow with you."

That's not performance. That's intimacy. It's what becomes possible when healing stops being a solo act and starts becoming a shared language. It doesn't mean the relationship is perfect. It doesn't mean you forget what happened. It means someone has chosen to *stand beside you honestly*, not just *benefit from your survival*.

You don't need everyone to come with you. But the ones who do — *truly do* — will help you build something the old patterns never could: a relationship grounded not in ritual, but in recognition.

And that is where the rebuilding begins.

Part III - Recovery and Reconstruction

Healing doesn't begin with fixing what's broken. It begins with learning how to sit with what broke — and why.

This part of the journey is not about heroism. It's not about mastery. It's about returning. Returning to yourself with less judgment. Returning to your body with more compassion. Returning to your story not to rewrite the past, but to remember that survival was never the end goal.

In the chapters ahead, you won't be asked to become someone new. You'll be invited to recognize the self that's been waiting beneath the performance — the self who has always deserved care, even when their rituals were confusing, destructive, or deeply human.

Recovery here is not defined by sobriety. It's defined by coherence — the slow, intentional process of choosing patterns that support the truth, rather than shield you from it. It's about making space for grief before demanding growth. It's about learning what safety actually feels like before asking yourself to change. And it's about building new rhythms that don't just prevent collapse, but *make living feel meaningful again.*

You are not expected to be ready.
You are only asked to be willing.

Willing to hold yourself with more honesty.
Willing to question the patterns you once called protection.
Willing to try — even if trying still includes falling.

Recovery isn't a staircase. It's a return to rhythm. And reconstruction isn't about going back — it's about choosing, for the first time, to build forward with care.

Chapter 7 - Before You Heal, You Grieve

Healing doesn't begin with insight. It begins with loss.

Not just the loss of the pattern or the behavior — but the loss of what that pattern was holding. The moment the addiction stops working isn't just a turning point. It's a death. A death of routine. Of control. Of coherence. And that death carries grief.

This grief doesn't always announce itself. It doesn't arrive with ceremony. Sometimes, it shows up as silence. As stillness. As a hollow sense that something familiar has gone missing — not because it was good, but because it was *yours*. The ritual may have hurt you. But it also structured your days. Regulated your nights. It was what you reached for when nothing else helped. And now it's gone, or fading, or failing — and you're left with the space it used to occupy.

That space is not freedom. Not yet.
It's *emptiness*.
And that emptiness hurts.

But it's also honest.

This chapter isn't about moving on. It's not about silver linings or motivational reframes. It's about staying long enough to feel what's underneath the collapse — the sadness, the confusion, the quiet relief you're not ready to name. It's about mourning the version of you who did what they had to do to survive. It's about letting go without shame.

Before you heal, you grieve.
Because healing without grief is just pretending.
And you've done enough of that already.

7.1

Naming the Loss

Grief is not just something that arrives after healing.
Often, it's what makes healing possible.

But the grief that surfaces in recovery is rarely simple. It's
not clean, not linear, not just about what's ending. It's
layered. Disorienting. It carries with it not just the pain of
the behavior you're letting go of, but the ache of
everything that behavior was holding together.

There are two griefs.

The first grief came long before the addiction. It lived
beneath your skin, often unnamed. It was the grief of what
you didn't receive — not dramatically, perhaps, but
consistently. The love that came with conditions. The
safety that never arrived. The spaces where you were seen
only when you were useful. This grief is quiet, but deep. It
forms early and settles in. Not because you weren't strong,
but because strength was the only thing you were allowed
to show.

That grief didn't go away. You just found a way to survive
it.

And that survival had structure. It had form. It had
rhythm. It became the second thing you're grieving now:
the addiction itself — the behavior, the pattern, the ritual
that stepped in where care should have been. The thing
that helped you get through the nights. The thing that
numbed the ache just enough to keep going. The thing
that didn't heal the wound, but wrapped it in something
familiar.

Letting go of that structure feels like progress from the outside. But inside, it can feel like devastation. Not because the addiction was good. But because it was yours. Because it worked — for a while. And now, without it, you're left with the original grief *and* the loss of the thing that protected you from feeling it.

This is why recovery often begins in emotional freefall. Because when the structure falls away, there's nothing left between you and the truth. And the truth isn't always kind. It's not always beautiful. Sometimes it's just cold and silent and heavy with memories of what you never had — and what you no longer know how to hold.

Aside: The Grace in Seeing Clearly

The truth may not feel kind or beautiful at first — but the ability to see it, to hold it without fleeing, and to choose growth anyway becomes its own kind of beauty.
Not the aesthetic kind.
The sacred kind.
The kind that comes from recognizing your own humanity and meeting it with grace, not judgment.
The kind that whispers: *You don't need to be better to be worthy. You only need to be honest.*

But that silence is also honest. It doesn't lie to you like the ritual did. It doesn't promise to erase the pain or make you whole overnight. It simply asks you to name what was lost — both the original wound and the architecture you built to survive it.

And naming it matters.

Not to blame yourself. Not to blame the behavior. But to say, *This is what I carried. This is what helped me. This is what it cost me.* Because without naming it, grief becomes shame. And without grief, healing becomes performance.

You don't have to let go all at once. You don't even have to be ready to let go. But if you can begin to name what was never offered to you — and what you built to endure that absence — you've already taken the first honest step.

Not toward perfection. Not toward resolution.
But toward coherence.
And that's where the real work begins.

7.2

Grieving the Self You Became

There's a particular kind of grief that doesn't show up in funerals or photo albums. It doesn't come with condolences or commemorative rituals. It's quiet. Inward. Hard to explain. It's the grief of realizing that the version of yourself you became — the one you had to become to survive — was never who you were meant to be.

This isn't shame, not at first. Shame says you were wrong. This grief says you were doing your best. And still — something was lost in the process. The loss wasn't always obvious. Sometimes it looked like success. Sometimes it looked like ruin.

You may have become someone who smiled brightly while falling apart inside. Someone who stayed productive, accommodating, driven — not because it brought you joy, but because it gave you control. You may have become the caretaker, the fixer, the person everyone leaned on. The one who made their pain useful and never asked to have your own witnessed. You might've survived by being excellent — or by disappearing.

Or maybe you couldn't hold the mask. Maybe your survival didn't look like composure. Maybe it looked like chaos — like rage, like bingeing, like numbing, like carelessness that other people called self-destruction but was actually the only way you could feel anything. Maybe you spiraled not because you didn't care, but because caring had become unbearable. Maybe you failed not because you were lazy, but because pretending to be okay felt like the lie that might finally kill you.

These versions of self weren't mistakes. They were strategies. Both the polished and the wrecked. Both the functioning and the flailing. They got you through environments that never knew how to love you in your full complexity. They carried you through absence — of safety, of support, of real witnessing. And they worked, until they didn't.

At some point, the cracks began to show. The exhaustion. The emotional dissonance. The way people praised your resilience but never asked about the cost. The way relationships revolved around your usefulness or your damage — but rarely your truth. The way silence became your first language, or chaos became your only one. And in that quiet — or in that wreckage — maybe you started to wonder: *Who was I supposed to be, if I hadn't had to survive this way?*

That's where the grief lives.

It lives in the gap between your true self and the self the world demanded.

It lives in the roles you played so well that even you began to believe them.

It lives in the collapse you were punished for, even though it was just your body telling the truth.

It lives in the dreams you let die in order to stay here.

It lives in the anger at those who never saw the signs.

And it lives in the haunting realization that no one stopped you — because you were either *too good at hiding,* or *too far gone to matter.*

This grief doesn't ask for pity. It asks for permission — to feel, to rage, to mourn. It asks for time, for quiet, for enough self-compassion to stop performing pain or pretending it never happened. It asks you to look back without flinching and say: *You did what you had to do. I see you. I honor you. But you don't have to carry this anymore.*

You don't need to hate the person you became. They were resourceful. They were protective. They were, in many ways, heroic. But now, you are allowed to let them rest. To lay down the armor — whether it was smiling or spiraling — and begin again from something softer.

You are not grieving failure.

You are grieving disconnection.

And that grief is not a weakness — it is the first sign that you're ready to return.

Not to who you were.

But to the self who's been waiting for you beneath all the pretending, all the spiraling, all the survival.

The one who never stopped hoping there was something more than this.

Pause and Consider

Your grief was always yours to bear.

Others may have witnessed parts of it. Some may have offered empathy. Some may have ignored it. But none of them could live it for you — and none of them ever will.

That doesn't make you unworthy of comfort. It just means your healing was never meant to come from being externally understood or validated. It was always going to come from *understanding and validating yourself.*

You now know what running from grief does. It doesn't disappear. It festers. It spirals. It reshapes your life in ways you barely recognize — until you wake up one day and realize you've become someone you never meant to be.

But now you have a choice.

You can return to yourself. You can name the pain without apologizing for it. You can stop asking others to validate what you already know:

That your grief is real.
That your story matters.
That you deserve to stop running.

This is not just healing.
This is self-ownership.

And it's the beginning of autonomy — not the kind that rejects others, but the kind that finally includes you.

7.3

Making Room for Something New

In Western culture, most people don't recover until they've lost everything.

We don't talk about addiction until it explodes. We don't name pain until it's public. We don't take healing seriously until someone "hits rock bottom." Until the family steps in. Until the job is gone. Until the body breaks. Until the mask slips so far that no one can pretend anymore.

And even then, we treat recovery like a personal triumph — as if the collapse was a necessary initiation. As if suffering deeply enough is the price of admission for change.

This is the lie.

Addiction is not rare. It's cultural. It's common. It's built into the rhythms of how we cope, how we relate, how we stay afloat in systems that don't know how to hold us. And most people are suffering long before the crisis. Quietly. Chronically. Invisibly. They are showing up, performing "normal," while inside they are drowning in the rituals they no longer believe in.

The only reason change feels dramatic is because honesty is so rare.

The truth is, you may not need to hit bottom. You may already be in pain. You may already be waking up with a body that's tired of the loop. You may already feel the hollowness of the behavior that used to work. And maybe, for the first time, you're not asking, *How do I stop?*
You're asking, *What could begin if I stopped needing this?*

That's where real recovery starts. Not in collapse. In clarity.

Letting go doesn't need to be explosive. It doesn't have to arrive with ultimatums or interventions. It can begin with discomfort. With restlessness. With that sick, dull awareness that your life has started to revolve around something that no longer serves you. And that whisper — that *this can't be it* — is a signal. Not a failing.

But here's what most people don't tell you: you can't just let go. You have to make room.

Because the pattern wasn't just behavior. It was structure. It was emotional architecture. It filled the space where love and regulation and safety should have lived. And when it begins to fall away, what you're left with isn't peace. It's *vacancy*.

That vacancy must be honored — not rushed, not ignored, not patched over with a new fixation. It must be tended like grief. Like soil. Like the place where your next life might root itself, if you're willing to stop managing your pain and start witnessing it.

Making room means slowing down.
It means recognizing when the old story no longer fits — and not rushing to replace it.
It means asking, with terrifying honesty:
What was this pattern protecting me from? What truth have I been avoiding? And what would it take to build something that doesn't require me to suffer in secret?

Letting go isn't soft. It isn't tidy. It's not a feel-good moment for your memoir.
It's war with your former logic.
It's the beginning of autonomy.

And autonomy doesn't mean being alone.
It means being honest.

You are not abandoning the pattern.
You are confronting the truth that it was never your fault
you needed it —
and it is your responsibility now to build something that
doesn't cost you yourself.

Reflection Prompt

The following can be reflected upon in a journal, group
therapy, or individual therapy:

Think about the pattern you've been holding — the one
that once gave you relief, or control, or coherence.

What was it protecting you from?

What did it help you survive?

What have you lost by keeping it?

What might it look like to stop managing your pain and
start witnessing it?

If you could make room — not to fix yourself, but to
finally be yourself — what would you want to grow there?

Chapter 8 - Safety Before Sobriety

Sobriety is often presented as the first step. The proof of commitment. The litmus test for readiness. But for many people, sobriety — true, lasting sobriety — isn't possible until something far more foundational is in place: *safety*.

Because no matter how much willpower you summon, no matter how many mantras you repeat, if your nervous system still lives in a state of threat, you will reach for regulation in the fastest way you know. And for most of us, that's the old pattern.

This isn't failure. It's survival.

Addiction is not just about avoiding pain — it's about creating a sense of control in environments where your pain was never honored. If sobriety becomes just another demand — another place where you're expected to perform, succeed, or suffer through — it becomes indistinguishable from punishment. And what your body needs, more than anything, is permission to feel *safe enough to try something new.*

Safety doesn't mean comfort all the time. It doesn't mean freedom from struggle. It means your system no longer believes that collapse is the only option. It means your body stops bracing. Your mind starts trusting. It means that the need to numb doesn't override the desire to stay present.

This chapter is about that groundwork. The conditions required for true change — not just abstinence, but reconstruction. It's about co-regulation. About the role of environment. About trust, attachment, and the permission to slow down *before* you're asked to get clean, or clear, or better.

Because without safety, sobriety is just restraint.
And recovery should never feel like a cage.

8.1

What Safety Actually Means

Safety is one of those words that gets thrown around so often it loses its shape. We talk about "safe spaces," "feeling safe," "playing it safe." But in the context of recovery, safety isn't a metaphor. It's a biological requirement.

Safety, in this sense, isn't the absence of danger. It's the presence of coherence.

It's the felt sense that your body is no longer in a state of constant defense. That you don't have to brace for disappointment, rejection, or shame every time you show up in a room — or in your own mind. It's knowing, not intellectually but *viscerally*, that you are allowed to exist without performing, without protecting, without explaining.

For people who've lived in survival mode — especially those whose addiction began as a way to manage trauma, disconnection, or neglect — safety doesn't come naturally. It has to be learned. And before it can be learned, it has to be *unlearned* from everything it was mistaken for.

Because many of us were taught that safety meant silence. Compliance. Perfection. We were told we were "safe" when we weren't making anyone uncomfortable. When we didn't need anything. When we weren't visible in ways that challenged the people around us.

So when recovery asks us to *feel*, we panic. Because the body still believes that feeling means risk.

This is where the old patterns reassert themselves — not because we're weak, but because the nervous system doesn't know the difference between healing and threat until someone teaches it otherwise.

That's why sobriety cannot come first.

You cannot build a new rhythm on top of a system that's still bracing for attack. You cannot expect sobriety to stick when your mind is still living in the logic of war. What you need, first, is a context where your fear makes sense — and isn't punished. A space where your truth is witnessed before it is corrected. A room where your presence is welcome *even when you're messy, hurting, or unsure.*

What safety actually means is this:

You don't have to earn your right to exist.
You don't have to disappear to belong.
You don't have to be better to be held.

Only from there — only from *that* kind of safety — can sobriety become more than survival. It can become choice. Movement. Return.

Vignette: A Different Kind of Meeting

He didn't want to call. But the edge was creeping in again — that slow hum in his chest, the feeling that something was slipping. He hadn't used. Not yet. But the world felt too loud again, and he couldn't quite remember what he was supposed to do with himself when it did.

He texted instead. *"Can we meet? I think I need structure."*

The response came quickly. *"Absolutely. You pick the place."*

That part always threw him. He wasn't used to being the one who chose. For most of his life, help had come with terms. Rules. Programs. Expectations. Even in recovery, it sometimes felt like if he wasn't following the script, he was wasting someone's time.

But when his sponsor arrived, they didn't look rushed. Or concerned. Or calculating his progress in quiet disappointment. They just smiled and said, "Thanks for meeting me. You doing okay?"

He shrugged. "I don't know. Just... needed something."

They sat down. The place was crowded. Music in the background. Too many conversations overlapping. A table behind them laughed loudly — not at him, but his body didn't know the difference. His shoulders tensed. He stared into the menu like it could shield him.

His sponsor noticed. Didn't say anything at first. Just waited a few minutes. Let the moment breathe. Then, gently: "Hey... would it help to ask for a quieter table?"

He looked up. "I don't want to be a hassle."

"You're not," they said. No hesitation. "You're learning to listen to yourself. That's not a hassle. That's recovery."

He hesitated. "Yeah. I think I'd like that."

They flagged down a server. "Could we move somewhere with less noise? Just something a little more calm." No apology. No excuse. Just a simple request. The server nodded and smiled. A few minutes later, they were at a small booth in the back corner.

The shift was immediate. The lights were softer. The table smaller. His breath came easier.

"This is better," he said.

"I'm glad," the sponsor replied. "Let's remember this. *You made that call.* You noticed what you needed. You asked for it. That's safety, my friend. Not perfection. Not rules. Just presence — and room to make it yours."

He didn't cry. But something in his chest unclenched.

For the first time in days, he felt like he might stay.
Not because he had to.
Because *he wanted to.*

Pause and Consider

What does safety look like for *you?*

Not the kind others expected you to settle for. Not the kind that came with silence, performance, or earning your worth. The kind your body would recognize as *real.*

Is it quiet? Is it slow? Is it knowing you can speak without being interrupted? Is it not having to speak at all? Is it physical space? Predictability? Eye contact? Laughter? Stillness?

Take a moment to imagine it — fully, honestly. Let the picture be yours, even if it surprises you. Especially if it does.

Then, if you feel ready, share it with someone you trust.

And when you do, ask them: *What does safety look like for you?*

This is how we begin to build it together — not by assuming, but by asking. Not by managing others, but by meeting them.

Vulnerability is not just a gift you give. It's an invitation to return — to yourself, and to others — without performance.

Real safety is co-created.
And this is how it starts.

8.2

Co-Regulation and Why You Were Never Meant to Do This Alone

You were never supposed to carry this alone. That may feel foreign, even contradictory to everything you've been taught. For many, survival became synonymous with independence. From a young age, you may have been praised for not needing anything. For handling things on your own. For bouncing back quickly, pushing through quietly, or staying composed when others fell apart. But what looked like strength was often just the absence of support.

The human nervous system is not wired for isolation. From birth, we are biologically programmed to seek regulation through connection. A glance. A soft voice. A steady presence. These are not luxuries — they are instructions to the body: *You are safe here.* When those signals are missing, inconsistent, or paired with threat, our systems adapt. We don't stop needing safety; we start building it ourselves — however we can.

This is where addiction often begins. Not as a conscious choice, but as a structural improvisation. When emotional safety cannot be found in relationships, it is constructed through behavior. Ritual becomes a substitute for rhythm. Repetition becomes regulation. The pattern, whether substance-based or behavioral, mimics what co-regulation should have provided. It becomes the body's only reliable way to settle, to soften, to survive.

This is why recovery cannot be reduced to willpower or abstinence. Removing the behavior without replacing the structure leaves the nervous system in the same state of threat it was in to begin with. What's missing isn't discipline — it's *relationship*. Specifically, relationships that allow the nervous system to experience safety without performance.

Co-regulation does not mean dependency. It is not a collapse into others, nor is it a romanticized idea of being "healed by love." It is a basic biological reality: people need people to feel okay. Not all the time. Not in every moment. But predictably enough that the body can begin to loosen its grip on hypervigilance.

For many, this kind of connection has never existed. Relationships have been transactional or exhausting. Vulnerability has been punished. Emotional needs have been minimized or ignored. It's no wonder then that trust feels impossible. But safety is not trust. Safety is what makes trust *possible*.

Co-regulation looks like small, repeatable moments. Texting a friend before the spiral starts, not because they'll fix it, but because their presence helps you breathe. Asking someone to sit with you, not talk at you. Letting a sponsor, therapist, or chosen person be near your distress without you needing to explain it away. It's about being seen without being managed.

Recovery is not a solo act. No matter what cultural myths say about personal responsibility or pulling yourself up by your emotional bootstraps, healing happens in context. And context means people. When you find even one person who doesn't flinch at your honesty — who stays soft when you feel hard, who listens when you're incoherent, who welcomes you without needing you to be better — something starts to change.

Not immediately. Not all at once. But gradually, your system begins to learn that connection doesn't have to cost you your safety. And that lesson is the foundation for everything that comes next.

You don't need to be fixed before you're allowed to belong.
You don't need to be sober before you're allowed to feel held.
You just need one honest relationship where your body can learn: *I don't have to do this alone anymore.*

8.3

Co-Regulation Is Not Romance

In Western culture, we don't have many models for deep, platonic intimacy. Vulnerability tends to get channeled into one of two paths: romantic or therapeutic. You're either dating someone, or you're paying someone. Outside of those categories, real closeness is rare — and often misunderstood.

That's why co-regulation can feel confusing at first. When someone meets your emotional honesty with presence instead of discomfort — when they stay, when they soften, when they actually *see you* — something powerful shifts. But if you've never experienced that kind of safe, consistent connection without strings attached, your brain may do what it's been trained to do: assume this must be romantic. Or sexual. Or that the feelings it stirs up must mean something more.

This is not a flaw. It's conditioning.

Most of us weren't taught that closeness could be *just closeness.* That being witnessed could be enough. That another human being could meet you where you are —

tender, tired, undone — and not need anything in return. So when it happens, it can feel disorienting. It can trigger attraction, anxiety, confusion, even shame. For some, especially men raised in emotionally repressive environments, it can bring up fears around identity or masculinity. For others, it may raise questions about boundaries, intentions, or emotional safety.

But here's what matters: co-regulation is not about romance. It's about nervous system repair.

It's about relearning how to be with people without performing. It's about being emotionally seen without needing to sexualize, rescue, impress, or seduce. It's about building safety that doesn't collapse into expectation. And that takes practice — not because the concept is complicated, but because the culture you've lived in *made it rare*.

You might feel affection for the people you co-regulate with. You might feel gratitude so deep it borders on infatuation. That's normal. Your body is responding to the fact that it's being met in a way it was never taught to expect. But affection does not mean you owe or are owed a relationship. And resonance does not mean romance.

In fact, the healthiest co-regulation is built on clear, grounded, platonic connection. Boundaries are not walls — they're structure. They allow trust to form without distortion. They keep the space safe for both people, especially when emotions are high or needs are raw. Naming the space as platonic — even explicitly — can be one of the most liberating things you ever do in recovery.

And if you've never had that kind of connection before? That doesn't mean you've failed. It means you're right where you need to be: *at the beginning of something new.*

Recovery isn't about transferring dependence from a substance to a person. It's about replacing isolation with reciprocal presence — the kind that doesn't ask you to give more than you have, or be more than you are.

Co-regulation is where you learn that love doesn't have to cost your identity. That closeness doesn't require romance. And that safety doesn't need to be earned through performance — only respected through presence.

8.4

When Sex Wasn't About Sex

Sex addiction is one of the most misunderstood and stigmatized forms of addiction. It's often framed as a lack of control, a moral failing, or worse, a sign of broken character. But like every other compulsive pattern in this book, it's not just about the behavior. It's about what the behavior was trying to hold.

For many, sex — especially transactional sex — isn't driven by lust. It's driven by *longing.* The act itself may feel urgent, but the need underneath is far quieter: to be seen, touched, wanted, even if only for an hour. Especially for those who have never known what safe intimacy looks like, sex becomes a shortcut to connection. Not because the sex is healing, but because it's the only ritual they've known where vulnerability feels allowed — or at least, *negotiated.*

This is particularly true for people who pay for sex. What looks from the outside like indulgence is often something much more fragile: *an attempt to feel emotionally held without risking rejection.* The dynamic is clear. The expectations are outlined. There's no threat of judgment, no need to explain yourself. You show up, you're wanted — even if you paid to be.

That kind of structure can feel safer than the ambiguity of real connection.

It can feel safer than friendship.
Safer than dating.
Safer than asking someone to stay and not knowing if they will.

Sex addiction is rarely about sex. It's about regulation. It's about trying to soothe something wordless through something physical. It's about using the body to reach for a kind of emotional acknowledgment you were never given permission to need.

And yes, there can be fantasy. There can be compulsion. There can be patterns rooted in shame and secrecy. But beneath all of that, there is almost always a human being trying to feel less alone. Someone using the only language they were taught to ask for connection — even when it never actually worked.

This is why healing from sex addiction isn't just about abstaining from sex. It's about relearning what intimacy actually means. It's about slowly unlearning the story that your only value is in being desired. That your body is the only access point for closeness. That paying for connection is safer than risking real, reciprocal presence.

It's also about facing grief. The grief of what the sex never gave you. The grief of realizing that even the most intense moments didn't actually touch the part of you that was aching to be known. That the closeness was conditional. That the feeling faded the moment the room emptied out.

You're allowed to be honest about that.
You're allowed to say: *It wasn't about sex. I just didn't know how else to be close to someone without being destroyed by it.*

That's not shameful. That's a nervous system doing its best to survive emotional isolation.

You don't need to punish yourself for how you reached for connection.
You just need a new way to find it.
One that starts with being safe enough in your own body to be seen — not bought.

Pause and Consider

Take a moment to reflect on how emotional closeness was modeled for you growing up.

When you needed comfort, who showed up?
When you were scared, who held space — not with solutions, but with presence?
When you expressed pain, were you met with tenderness, or silence? Control? Confusion?

If your answers are hard to name, you're not alone.
If the idea of "healthy intimacy" feels unfamiliar — even threatening — you're not broken.

For many, sex addiction is not about craving sex. It's about seeking a kind of contact that was never safe, but was learned through unwanted touch that may have been as simple as not being allowed to say no to hugs — or as serious as sexual assault. If your earliest experiences of touch, affection, or closeness were tangled with harm — manipulation, coercion, or abuse — your nervous system may have learned to associate intimacy with danger, control, or guilt.

If this section stirred something painful or confusing in you — *something older than your behavior* — you are not imagining it. And you don't have to make sense of it alone.

Consider reaching out to a therapist, trauma-informed recovery group, or survivor network. Not because you need fixing — but because what happened to you was never your fault. And your healing doesn't have to be, either.

Recovery is not just about stopping what hurts.
It's about learning how to be held safely — for the very first time.

8.5

Sobriety as Capacity, Not Identity

Sobriety is often treated as a finish line. A title. A badge of honor that proves you've done the work. The longer you've abstained, the more seriously you're taken. The more "real" your recovery is assumed to be. But in that framing, sobriety becomes something rigid — something you either are, or are not. And the moment you slip, everything you've built is called into question.

This is the trap of identity-based sobriety. It takes a process that should be adaptive, human, and evolving — and turns it into a binary: you're either succeeding or failing. Clean or using. Sober or broken. And in that binary, there's no room for honesty, no room for nuance, and certainly no room for compassion.

But what if sobriety wasn't about identity?
What if it was about *capacity*?

Capacity is the space you have, in a given moment, to make choices aligned with your values. It is shaped by your nervous system. By your environment. By how supported or threatened you feel. Some days, your capacity is wide — you have access to your tools, your relationships, your regulation. Other days, your capacity shrinks — not because you've lost progress, but because your system is under strain.

When sobriety is defined by capacity, relapse is no longer framed as failure. It's framed as data. A message from your body: *I ran out of space.* And that message deserves inquiry, not shame.

What was missing that day?
What wasn't available?
What needed to be felt that you couldn't hold alone?

This framing also removes sobriety from the center of your identity. You are not "a sober person." You are a person in recovery, building the capacity to live without the ritual that once held your pain. You are learning new rhythms. New ways of regulating. New ways of being witnessed without collapsing into performance or control.

And in that process, sobriety becomes *less about proving something to others* and more about listening to yourself. Am I safe enough right now to choose something else? Do I have the support I need? Do I feel regulated enough to not reach for the old rhythm?

Sobriety, in this light, is a *byproduct* — not a performance. It emerges when the system is resourced. When connection is present. When shame is low and self-trust is rising. It isn't always clean or continuous. But it becomes more possible when you stop defining it as proof of your worth.

You don't owe anyone a perfect record.
You owe yourself the right to build a life where staying feels like something you *want*, not something you *must*.

And that begins when you stop treating sobriety like an identity you have to protect — and start treating it like the capacity you are slowly reclaiming.

Chapter 9 – Trauma & Addiction

Before addiction becomes behavior, it is biology.

Before it is choice, it is adaptation.

This chapter is not about morality, nor about willpower, nor about the cultural debates that so often surround addiction. It is about structure — about what happens inside a nervous system that has learned to survive without safety.

When the body lives too long in threat, it does not simply "move on." It reorganizes. Stress responses become baseline states. Hypervigilance becomes normal. Emotional flooding or emotional numbness replaces steady regulation. The system never returns fully to rest. And when that happens, the person is left with a problem that is rarely named: they must find a way to feel stable in a body that no longer knows how.

This is where addiction enters the picture — not as rebellion, not as indulgence, but as engineering. A regulatory solution constructed under pressure. A way to compress emotion, to narrow chaos into something repeatable, predictable, controllable. In the absence of reliable co-regulation — the steadying presence of others who can help a nervous system settle — the person builds containment alone.

That containment often takes the form of ritual. Repetition. Substance. Behavior. Something that works, at least for a time. Something that provides a sense of coherence when the internal world feels fragmented. In this light, addiction is not random. It is not evidence of weak character. It is a predictable adaptation in systems shaped by chronic dysregulation and relational failure — a survival structure doing the best it can with the tools available.

Understanding addiction this way changes the questions we ask. Instead of "Why can't they stop?" we begin to ask, "What was this behavior stabilizing?" Instead of seeing only destruction, we begin to see design — a nervous system trying to hold itself together after safety was never fully established, or long ago lost.

This chapter explores that design. Not to excuse harm, but to explain it. Not to romanticize suffering, but to map the terrain. Because until we understand how the system adapted, we cannot know what it truly needs to heal.

9.1

Trauma as Regulatory Disruption

We tend to talk about trauma as if it lives in the event — in the explosion, the accident, the assault, the moment that can be pointed to and named. But the nervous system does not organize experience by narrative clarity. It organizes by threat and safety. From that perspective, trauma is not defined by how dramatic something looks from the outside. Trauma is defined by what happens inside the body afterward.

Trauma occurs when activation does not resolve. When the system mobilizes for danger — heart rate up, breath shallow, muscles ready, attention narrowed — but never fully returns to baseline. The alarm was sounded, but the "all clear" never came. The body remains braced, scanning, prepared. Over time, this state stops feeling like a reaction and starts feeling like reality.

In post-traumatic stress disorder (PTSD), this dysregulation often shows up in episodes. Something triggers memory or sensation, and the system surges into activation again — panic, rage, shutdown, dissociation. There may be periods of relative calm, but the return to baseline is fragile, easily disrupted. The person lives with a nervous system that can be thrown back into emergency mode by cues others might not even notice.

Complex post-traumatic stress (C-PTSD) follows a different pattern. Here, dysregulation is not an interruption to development — it is the environment development occurs within. The child or adult does not have a before-and-after experience of safety. Instead, identity forms inside chronic unpredictability. Emotional containment is inconsistent or absent. Repair after distress is unreliable. The system grows up learning that activation is normal, that vigilance is necessary, that relaxation is risky.

In both cases, the core problem is the same: the nervous system has lost reliable access to safety. It does not know how to stand down. It does not trust stillness. And when a system cannot find safety naturally, it must find it artificially.

This is the key shift. The nervous system that never returned to safety will attempt to construct safety. Not philosophically. Not symbolically. Physiologically. It will search for patterns that reduce unpredictability, narrow overwhelming emotional states, and create a sense of control. It will favor repetition, routine, and anything that produces a temporary drop in internal chaos.

That search happens against a backdrop of ongoing dysregulation. Hypervigilance becomes a default state — constant scanning for threat, difficulty relaxing, startle responses that feel out of proportion but are deeply conditioned. Emotional flooding may follow, where feelings arrive too quickly and too intensely to process, leaving the person overwhelmed, reactive, or ashamed of reactions they do not fully understand. At other times, the opposite occurs: collapse states. The system shuts down to conserve energy, producing numbness, disconnection, fatigue, and a sense of being absent from one's own life.

As these patterns repeat, something else begins to erode: self-coherence. When a person swings between hyperarousal and shutdown, between emotional intensity and emotional absence, it becomes harder to maintain a stable sense of who they are. Reactions feel foreign. Memory fragments. Identity begins to organize around managing states rather than expressing self. Life becomes less about meaning and more about regulation.

This is the terrain addiction enters. Not as an abstract moral failure, but as a solution to a regulation problem. When the nervous system cannot reliably create safety through rest, relationship, or internal stability, it looks elsewhere. It looks for something that works on demand — something that can compress emotion, dull activation, create predictability, or simulate control. Addiction is one such answer.

9.2

Co-Regulation: The Missing Architecture

To understand why addiction becomes such an elegant — and costly — solution, we have to look at what should have been in place long before the behavior ever appeared.

Human beings do not learn regulation alone.

From the beginning, our nervous systems are social. An infant cannot calm itself through logic or self-talk. It does not breathe slowly on purpose or reframe its thoughts. Instead, it borrows regulation. A caregiver's tone of voice, facial expression, touch, and rhythm of movement all act as external regulators. The adult nervous system absorbs the child's distress, modulates it, and returns it in a form the child can tolerate. Over thousands of these small exchanges, the child's system gradually internalizes the pattern. What was once borrowed becomes built-in.

This is co-regulation. It is not sentimental. It is structural. Safety is relational before it is internal.

Emotional containment, in this sense, is co-created. Feelings move through one person and are steadied by another. Overwhelm is not faced in isolation but held in shared space. The child learns, without needing language, that activation can rise and fall, that distress can be survived, that emotional states are not permanent emergencies. This becomes the foundation for self-regulation later in life.

But when co-regulation is inconsistent, unsafe, or absent, that architecture never fully forms. The child's emotions have nowhere to go. Distress does not meet a steadying presence; it meets confusion, dismissal, unpredictability, or threat. Instead of being processed, emotional energy accumulates. The system remains activated — not because the person is dramatic or fragile, but because there has been no reliable pathway for discharge.

Over time, this accumulation reshapes experience. Stress becomes chronic rather than episodic. Emotional responses feel disproportionate because they are carrying old, unprocessed load. And identity coherence begins to weaken. If a person's internal world is dominated by unmanaged states — fear, shame, numbness, rage, collapse — it becomes harder to experience themselves as stable or continuous. They become someone who is "too much," or "not enough," or "hard to be with," without fully understanding why.

In the absence of relational containment, the system still seeks containment. The need does not disappear simply because the environment failed to meet it.

This is the pivot point:

When relational containment fails, internal containment must be constructed.

The nervous system does not accept chaos as a permanent condition. It searches for substitutes. Patterns, rituals, substances, behaviors — anything that can narrow emotional intensity and create predictability — begin to take on regulatory value. What should have been built through thousands of small relational exchanges is instead engineered through repetition and control.

Addiction grows in this gap.

There is another layer to this, one that is less visible but deeply consequential: not everyone begins life with a stable regulatory template available to borrow.

Caregivers themselves carry nervous systems shaped by their own histories. When a parent is chronically dysregulated — anxious, shut down, volatile, emotionally absent, or overwhelmed — the child is not borrowing stability. They are borrowing instability. Regulation is still happening socially, but the pattern being internalized is one of persistent activation or collapse. The child learns not what safety feels like, but what survival feels like.

This is how dysregulation can be inherited without being genetic in the narrow sense. It is transmitted through interaction — through tone, pacing, what is modeled, and what is missing. A caregiver who cannot down-regulate cannot reliably help a child down-regulate. Emotional states remain intense, confusing, or uncontained, and the nervous system adapts accordingly. Hypervigilance, numbing, people-pleasing, withdrawal — these become forms of social survival, learned early and carried forward.

Over time, this shapes what we often label as "emotional maturity," though that phrase can be misleading. Emotional maturity is not a moral achievement. It is the gradual internalization of regulation — the ability to experience strong affect without fragmentation, to remain in relationship during discomfort, to recover from stress without extreme compensatory behaviors. These capacities are built through repeated co-regulated experiences across development, and they do not arrive on a fixed timeline.

Many young adults — and many adults well into midlife — are still in the process of internalizing regulation because the conditions required for that internalization were inconsistent, delayed, or absent. The social architecture that should have supported emotional development may be physically distant, emotionally unavailable, or structurally fractured. Extended family networks are smaller. Community bonds are weaker. Mobility separates people from long-term relational anchors.

And this separation matters.

Moving away from regulating environments — from the people whose presence once stabilized the nervous system — can unmask dysregulation that had been quietly buffered. A service member leaving their unit, a physician relocating for work, an adult moving away from long-standing relationships may suddenly find themselves without the subtle co-regulation they had depended on without realizing it. The stress does not increase only because of new responsibilities; it increases because the nervous system is now managing alone.

In this context, dysregulation is not a sign of failure. It is a sign that the system is doing what it has always done: searching for stability with the resources available.

When relational regulation is too distant to access, or never fully internalized, the need for containment does not diminish. It intensifies. Emotional states still rise. Stress still accumulates. Identity still strains under the load. And without accessible relational scaffolding, the person turns inward to build structure through repetition, control, and sensory modulation.

Addiction becomes one form of that structure — not because the person lacks character, but because the regulatory architecture that might have made addiction unnecessary was never fully installed.

Vignette 1 – Group-Contained Trauma

Part I: The Environment

The hospital does not feel like a place of healing anymore. It feels like a perimeter.

It is early in the pandemic. Information changes by the hour. Protocols are rewritten between shifts. No one knows exactly how the virus spreads, how long it lingers, who will crash and who will walk out. Masks are reused. Protective equipment is rationed. Hallways are too quiet and too loud at the same time — the mechanical rhythm of ventilators layered over the absence of families who are no longer allowed inside.

Beds fill faster than they empty. Staff move from room to room carrying an awareness that does not turn off: this patient may not make it, that one probably won't, and the next admission is already waiting. Death is not unusual in a hospital, but this feels different. It is constant. It is anticipatory. It hovers.

Fear is present, but it does not look like panic. It looks like focus sharpened too tight. Movements become efficient, clipped. Conversations are brief and coded. Everyone is watching everyone else for signs of exposure, fatigue, or emotional slip. Hands are washed until skin cracks. Faces are marked by masks that stay on too long.

Outside the hospital, the world has slowed. Streets are quiet. Families are isolating. But inside, intensity has increased. Time does not stretch; it compresses. Shifts blur together. Sleep becomes functional, not restorative. The nervous system remains on alert long after staff leave the building. The body carries the sound of alarms, the sight of monitors, the memory of faces behind oxygen masks.

153

This is not a single event. It is a sustained environment of threat and uncertainty. There is no clear beginning or end, only continuation. The nervous system adapts the way it does under chronic load: vigilance increases, emotional range narrows, and the capacity for reflective processing decreases. There is no space to fully feel what is happening, because the next task is already in front of you.

Individually, this level of exposure would be destabilizing. But here, it is shared. Everyone in the building is moving through the same field of tension. The fear does not belong to one person; it circulates through the unit, the floor, the shift. No one needs to explain what they saw that day. They assume the others saw something similar.

The trauma is collective. So is the adaptation.

Part II: The Workplace Social Field

Inside the unit, the tone shifts in ways that would be jarring to an outsider.

Humor becomes darker, faster, sharper. Jokes surface in moments that might otherwise be silent. A line about "frequent flyer lungs." A mock argument over who's "winning" the ventilator count that night. Exaggerated complaints about PPE as if it were a fashion crisis. Laughter breaks out suddenly, then stops just as fast when the next alarm sounds.

It is not cruelty. It is not indifference. It is compression.

The humor narrows the emotional field. It takes something too large to hold — fear, grief, helplessness — and shrinks it into a shared signal: I see this too. I'm still here. We're still functioning.

Conversations are blunt. Language loses its polish. They talk about bodily fluids, about exhaustion, about the strange dreams that follow double shifts. Someone admits they're scared to go home. Someone else says they stopped watching the news because they're already "living it." No one offers a formal reassurance. They nod. They understand.

Understanding is the currency here.

No one has to justify their fatigue or explain their irritability. No one is told they're overreacting. The emotional load that might feel isolating elsewhere is normalized here. A look across the nurses' station can say, *Same*. A raised eyebrow can say, *I know*. A sarcastic comment can say, *We're still in this together*.

Between tasks, there are small rituals. A shared snack. A moment leaning against the counter while charting. A quick exchange in the supply room that lingers just long enough to breathe differently. These pauses are brief, but they are not empty. They are micro-discharges — tiny reductions in internal pressure, made possible because someone else is present to witness the strain.

One night, after a patient codes in a way no one expected, a nurse sits in the break room and just stares. No tears. No words. Just stillness that feels wrong. Another nurse sits beside her, doesn't speak, just matches her breathing. After five minutes, the first nurse exhales and says, 'Okay.' That's it. They both stand and return to the floor.

Outside the hospital, public messaging emphasizes distance: isolate, separate, protect others by staying apart. Inside the unit, the logic feels inverted. They are already equally exposed. They have breathed the same air, touched the same surfaces, entered the same rooms. Risk is no longer abstract or individual. It is shared.

So their social world narrows around one another. They talk about seeing each other outside of work, about being in the same small circle. Not because they reject caution, but because their nervous systems register these colleagues as the only people who fully understand the environment they are living in. Safety, in this context, is not the absence of exposure. It is the presence of recognition.

The stress does not disappear in these interactions. But it moves. It circulates. It is not held by one person alone.

Without naming it, they are co-regulating. Each exchange, each joke, each shared glance absorbs a fraction of the load. The emotional pressure that might otherwise build silently inside one body is distributed across many.

The trauma is still there. But so is containment.

Part III: Off-Shift Regulation

When the shift ends, the nervous system does not.

The body leaves the building, but the activation comes along. Muscles stay tight. Thoughts move fast. Sleep, when it comes, is shallow. Images from the day replay in fragments — a monitor alarm, the weight of protective gear, a patient's eyes above a mask. The system remains braced, even in stillness.

Going home alone with that load can be disorienting. The quiet feels unnatural. Family members who are not inside the hospital do not fully understand the texture of the day. Questions are well-meaning but exhausting to answer. The gap between environments becomes visible.

So the staff gravitate toward one another.

They meet for drinks after late shifts. Someone hosts a small gathering on a night off. Text threads stay active well past midnight. The conversations echo the tone of the unit — blunt, irreverent, fast. Stories are told in shorthand. No one needs the background explained. The laughter is louder here, the exhaustion more visible.

Alcohol becomes a common presence. Not always heavy, not always dramatic, but consistent. A way to mark the end of the shift. A way to soften the edge of hypervigilance. A way to create a predictable transition from high activation to something closer to rest. One drink becomes two, then becomes routine. It is not framed as a problem. It is framed as decompression.

Physical intimacy sometimes follows similar lines. Relationships form quickly. Boundaries blur. Shared exposure, shared stress, and shared recognition create a sense of closeness that feels immediate and unquestioned. Connection here is not abstract; it is embodied. Being near someone who has been in the same rooms, breathed the same air, seen the same suffering can feel stabilizing in a way that is hard to describe outside the group.

Over time, an in-group identity solidifies. There are inside jokes, shared references, a sense of "us" that contrasts sharply with the outside world. Public conversations about safety measures, politics, or fear can feel distant or misaligned with their lived experience. Within the group, the narrative is different: *We know what this is. We've been there. We're still standing.*

These off-shift rituals do more than fill time. They extend the co-regulation that began in the hospital. Emotional load continues to be distributed across multiple nervous systems. The drink is not the only regulator in the room. Neither is the sexual connection. The group itself is regulating — through presence, recognition, shared language, and repetition.

This does not mean the behaviors are harmless. It does not mean long-term consequences are absent. But it changes how we understand them. What looks like indulgence from the outside often functions, from the inside, as a continuation of distributed containment. The alcohol narrows the emotional field. The closeness counters isolation. The in-group identity restores coherence after a day of fragmentation.

The key difference is this: the regulation is not happening in isolation. The compression of emotion is buffered by shared experience. The nervous system is not carrying the load alone.

This is why collapse risk is often lower in these group-contained environments, even when addiction-like behaviors are present. Stress discharge is ongoing, if imperfect. Identity remains anchored in belonging. Recognition reduces fragmentation.

The trauma is severe. The coping is messy. But the regulation is social.

9.3

Regulatory Isolation

The same nervous system placed in a different environment can produce a very different outcome.

When trauma is shared, emotional load circulates. It moves between people, carried in glances, humor, recognition, and ritual. But when trauma is carried alone, there is nowhere for the excess activation to go.

No mirroring.

No one who instinctively understands the internal landscape. Reactions feel exaggerated, private, hard to explain. Emotional states that might have been normalized in a group now feel like personal defects. The person begins to monitor themselves instead of being steadied by others.

No discharge.

Stress still rises, but there are no micro-moments of shared exhale. No supply room conversations. No dark humor that shrinks the unbearable into something briefly manageable. Activation accumulates quietly. Sleep does not reset the system. The body remains in a state of unresolved readiness.

No narrative integration.

Experience piles up without being metabolized into story. Events remain sensory fragments rather than shared meaning. Without conversation that says this happened to us, experience becomes this is happening to me. The difference is subtle but profound. Shared narrative distributes memory; isolation concentrates it.

No identity reinforcement.

In group-contained trauma, identity is buffered by belonging — nurse, medic, unit member, colleague. Recognition from others helps hold continuity when internal states fluctuate. In isolation, identity thins. The person becomes organized around managing symptoms rather than inhabiting a role or shared purpose. Life narrows to getting through the day, then the evening, then the night.

Under these conditions, the regulatory problem does not disappear. It intensifies.

The nervous system still needs containment. It still seeks predictability, narrowing of emotional intensity, and relief from chronic activation. But now there are no distributed supports. No shared nervous systems absorbing part of the load.

So the work falls inward.

Ritual becomes more rigid. Substances become more central. Behaviors that once supplemented social regulation begin to replace it. The drink is no longer just a marker of transition after a shift; it becomes the primary means of shifting states. The routine becomes less flexible. The behavior carries more weight.

Addiction becomes load-bearing when relational regulation disappears.

What once functioned as one regulator among many becomes the regulator. Emotional compression is no longer buffered by recognition, conversation, or belonging. The nervous system leans more heavily on whatever reliably narrows the field of experience. Relief comes, but at a cost: tolerance increases, options decrease, and the person's world organizes increasingly around maintaining the one structure that still works.

From the outside, this can look like escalation, loss of control, or moral decline. From the inside, it is a system under strain, assigning more responsibility to the only mechanism that consistently delivers a change in state.

The difference between shared trauma and isolated trauma is not the presence of stress. It is the availability of regulation.

162

Vignette: The Isolated Veteran

Part I: The Field

The blast is not loud at first. It is pressure — a force that lifts the air and shoves it sideways. Sound comes after, thick and distant, as if underwater.

Dust closes the world down to brown and gray. He tastes dirt and metal. Someone is shouting but the words don't land. His hands are already moving before he feels them move. Rifle up. Scan. Return fire. The ground is wrong under his knees — soft where it shouldn't be.

He calls names. No answer. Calls again, louder. The radio crackles, then cuts, then crackles again. Training moves his body through the motions: drag, cover, check, move. One shape does not move. Another is too still. There is no space to stop.

He takes position behind fractured concrete and aims at the ridge line where the shots came from. The world narrows to the arc of his sight. Breath shallow. Jaw locked. Every muscle waiting for the next flicker of motion.

Time stretches.

Seconds do not pass. They hang. The sun shifts, barely. The air smells like burned wiring and hot stone. His heart does not slow. It hammers against the inside of his ribs like it is trying to leave.

He keeps the position because leaving it means someone else dies.

He does not feel fear the way movies show it. There is no panic, no screaming inside. There is only focus sharpened past comfort, past thought. Every sound is threat. Every silence is worse.

He does not look back at the bodies again.

He waits.

A sound from behind startles him and he turns to address the threat — firing almost before thinking.

A child with a bomb strapped to them lays dead where the sound emerged.

He flees in search of a new position as the bomb on the child explodes. Debris flies in all directions. The sound again reducing the world to a whistling hum inside his head.

He waits.

Extraction finally comes in noise and rotor wash. The sudden movement feels unreal, like stepping out of a photograph. Hands pull him up, voices too loud, too fast. Someone grips his shoulder and says something that might be praise, might be confirmation. He nods because nodding is easier than speaking.

The vehicle lifts. The ground shrinks. The position he held becomes landscape again.

His body is still on the ridge by the edge of the village.

Part II: The Return

The story begins to change as soon as the aircraft lands.

The language becomes clean. Efficient. Contained.

He is debriefed in a room with fluorescent lights and a table that has seen too many elbows. Questions come in sequence: location, timing, line of sight, ammunition count, movement of the patrol. He answers them. His voice sounds normal to his own ears, which feels like an accomplishment.

No one asks what stayed with him.

No one asks what did not leave.

There is praise. Not excessive, but enough. A hand on the shoulder. A nod from someone with rank. Words like steady and professional float past him. The narrative organizes itself around performance — what he did right, how the position was held, how extraction was secured.

The bodies become "losses."

The child becomes "a threat neutralized."

The ridge becomes "the site."

Language smooths the terrain.

Before he leaves, someone mentions resources. A pamphlet appears. A briefing slide about stress reactions. A tone that signals both availability and distance: Reach out if you need to. The words are correct. The room is not built for what they are offering.

He nods again.

He has learned the difference between what is asked and what is welcome. The system is built to restore function, not to hold collapse. The unspoken rule is clear: process later, privately, if at all. For now, stay operational.

So the event is filed as memory, but not metabolized. The story is told in ways that fit the structure around him. The parts that do not fit remain in the body.

He returns to routine with a nervous system that has not stood down.

Sleep comes in fragments. Noise enters him too quickly. Silence stretches too long. The world outside the base feels strangely thin, as if depth has been reduced. People talk about ordinary things with an ease that feels distant.

He is told he did well.

There is no place for what did not.

Part III: Home

Home is quiet in a way that feels unnatural.

The refrigerator hum is too loud. The house settles at night and the small sounds arrive like signals. He walks through rooms that have not changed and feels like he is visiting someone else's life. The walls are intact. The windows are clear. Nothing here requires him to scan the horizon.

His body does anyway.

Family members speak softly at first, then normally, then with relief. They are careful with questions. He is careful with answers. He offers pieces that fit inside a living room — the heat, the weight of the gear, the boredom between movements. He leaves the ridge out. He leaves the child out. He leaves the moment of turning, firing, and knowing too late out.

At night, when the house goes still, the missing parts arrive.

Not as story. As flashes. The shape on the ground. The sound that came after. The knowledge that the threat and the child occupied the same body. There is no language for that in his world. Only the word necessary, repeated until it loses meaning.

He has a child of his own.

A small body in pajamas moves down the hallway one night, half asleep, calling his name. The sound lands wrong in his chest. He answers too quickly, voice sharper than he intends. The child blinks at him, confused. He softens, kneels, holds them. His hands shake. The thought arrives broken: *not the same not the same but what if what if.* He hates himself for the reflex.

From that night on, the child is both present and doubled. His own and not. Innocence and threat share a space in his mind he cannot separate. He watches longer than needed. He startles at sudden movement. He hates himself for the reflex.

There is nowhere to put this.

The system around him recognizes medals, not moral fracture. Conversations circle duty, sacrifice, pride. He nods at the right moments. The story others hold about him is clean. The one he holds is not.

The pressure builds quietly.

So he creates a boundary he can control.

A drink at night becomes a line between the day and what follows. The first swallow brings a softening — the edge dulls, the images lose sharpness, the body lowers by degrees. The second brings distance. The third brings quiet.

He tells himself it helps him sleep.

It does, at first.

The ritual becomes precise. Same glass. Same chair. Same hour. The drink does not ask him to explain himself. It does not look at him with pride or confusion. It does not require the story to be cleaned up.

It narrows the field.

No one sees this part. During the day he is steady, present, functional. He shows up. He performs the role that was handed back to him when he landed.

At night, alone, he contains what has no container.

The alcohol does what the system around him cannot: it compresses the unshared weight into something he can hold without breaking posture.

It works.

Until it doesn't.

Developmental Parallel: C-PTSD in Children

The same regulatory principles that shape trauma responses in adults are at work much earlier in life, but with a crucial difference: children do not yet have the internal architecture required to regulate themselves.

Self-regulation is not innate. It is built over time through repeated co-regulated experiences. Infants and young children depend on caregivers not only for physical safety, but for nervous system stabilization. When a child is distressed, overwhelmed, frightened, or confused, they require an external nervous system to help bring their activation back down. This happens through touch, voice, eye contact, rhythm, and repair after or during dysregulation. Over thousands of small interactions, children gradually internalize these patterns and develop the capacity to soothe, organize, and understand their own emotional states.

When this process is consistent enough, emotional development unfolds alongside neurological maturation. The child learns that distress has a beginning, middle, and end. They learn that feelings can be tolerated, that rupture can be repaired, and that they are not alone in moments of overwhelm. This is the foundation of what we later describe as emotional resilience or maturity.

But when co-regulation is inconsistent, unavailable, or confusing, development occurs under different conditions.

Children in these environments are not necessarily exposed to dramatic events. Trauma in childhood is not defined primarily by magnitude. It is defined by containment. A child's nervous system becomes destabilized not only by violence or disaster, but by repeated experiences of being emotionally alone in states they cannot manage.

Chronic compression and misattunement of dysregulation is one pathway. When caregivers frequently misread, dismiss, or fail to respond to a child's emotional signals, the child receives the message that their internal states are not reliably understood. Emotional experiences become isolating rather than shared. The child may learn to suppress feelings to preserve connection, or to amplify them in an effort to be seen, but in either case the regulation process is disrupted.

Emotional invalidation functions similarly. When distress is minimized, mocked, punished, or treated as an inconvenience, the child's emotional experience becomes something to manage privately. Instead of learning that feelings can move through relationship, the child learns that feelings are burdensome or unsafe to express. Activation remains inside the system.

Communication failure adds another layer. Children rely on language development not only to describe experience, but to organize it. When emotional states are not named, explained, or discussed in ways the child can understand, experiences remain sensory and confusing. Fear, shame, or anger may be felt intensely without context or resolution. The nervous system remains activated without integration.

Under these conditions, the same pattern seen in adult trauma begins to form: activation without reliable return to baseline. The child's system adapts by finding ways to create predictability and containment independently. These adaptations may not look like addiction at first. They may look like repetitive behaviors, rigid routines, fantasy immersion, sensory seeking, withdrawal, or early reliance on food, screens, or self-soothing habits. But the underlying logic is the same.

The child is solving a regulation problem.

Because children begin with less internal capacity, the threshold for destabilization is lower. Experiences that might be manageable for a well-regulated adult can be overwhelming for a child without consistent co-regulation. Over time, these early adaptations can solidify into the kinds of repetitive, state-altering behaviors we later recognize as addiction.

This is not a failure of character or parenting in a moral sense. It is a description of how nervous systems develop under different relational conditions. The logic that drives addiction in adulthood — the search for containment in the absence of sufficient co-regulation — is already visible in childhood, shaped by the environments in which regulation was, or was not, made possible.

When early regulatory architecture develops under conditions of chronic misattunement, invalidation, or emotional isolation, the effects do not disappear when childhood ends. They evolve.

By adolescence and early adulthood, the individual has more autonomy but not necessarily more internal stability. Emotional intensity may be high, but the capacity to process and discharge that intensity safely may still be limited. The person often does not experience themselves as "traumatized." They experience themselves as overwhelmed, restless, numb, reactive, or hard to settle.

The nervous system is still attempting to solve the same problem it faced earlier: how to manage activation without reliable co-regulation.

This can take multiple forms, sometimes in the same person at different times.

Risk-taking behavior can function as regulation. High stimulation narrows attention and overrides internal chaos. Speed, danger, intensity, or thrill can produce a temporary sense of clarity and aliveness. The person may describe feeling "more like myself" in high-risk situations, not because they seek harm, but because heightened external input organizes an otherwise disorganized internal state.

Risk aversion, paradoxically, can serve a similar regulatory purpose. Avoiding unfamiliar situations, social exposure, or emotional vulnerability reduces unpredictability. The world is narrowed to what feels manageable. Control replaces exploration. This can look like anxiety or rigidity, but structurally it is another attempt to reduce activation through predictability.

Self-harm behaviors often emerge from the same regulatory logic. Physical sensation can interrupt emotional flooding or dissociation. Pain, in this context, is not sought for punishment but for grounding — a way to locate the body and narrow overwhelming internal experience.

Rebellion and oppositional behavior can also reflect dysregulated systems. When internal states feel chaotic, external structure imposed by others can feel intolerable. Acting against authority can create a sense of agency and momentary coherence. Conflict provides focus. Defiance organizes emotion that otherwise feels diffuse.

In each case, the surface behavior differs, but the underlying function is similar: the person is trying to regulate nervous system states without sufficient internalized tools. They are searching for intensity, control, sensation, or predictability in ways that temporarily reduce internal chaos.

Over time, some of these strategies become more efficient than others. Substances, compulsive behaviors, or rigid routines may provide more consistent state change than thrill-seeking or avoidance alone. What began as varied attempts at regulation can narrow into the repetitive, ritualized patterns we recognize as addiction.

Seen this way, early adulthood behaviors that are often framed as irresponsibility, immaturity, or poor choices can be understood as extensions of developmental adaptation. The nervous system continues to work with the architecture it has. Without new relational experiences that support deeper regulation, earlier survival strategies simply take adult form.

Vignette: Holding Myself, a Child

Part I: The Child

The room is quiet except for the soft sounds from the tablet in the child's hands. The glow from the screen lights their face in shifting colors. Their body is still, breath even, attention narrowed. Outside the room, voices move through the house — dishes, footsteps, a door closing. The child hears it all, but the sounds are distant. The screen holds the edges of the world in place.

Inside the game, rules are clear. Inputs produce predictable outcomes. Characters respond the same way each time. The child knows what will happen next. Their body softens in ways no one notices.

From the hallway, the parent's voice arrives sharp and sudden.

"Put that away. Now!"

The child startles. The tablet drops slightly in their hands. Their heart jumps before their mind catches up. They look up, eyes wide, unsure what changed.

"I said now! You've been on that thing all day. Why don't you ever listen?!"

The words come fast. Irritation layered over exhaustion layered over something the child cannot see. The device is pulled from their hands. The room feels larger and less defined. The child's body stiffens, then shrinks inward. Their face goes blank.

From the parent's perspective, this is about limits. About balance. About correcting a habit.

From the child's nervous system, something else just happened.

The screen was not only entertainment. It was structure. Predictability. A narrow channel for overwhelming sensation. The sudden removal is not experienced as guidance; it is experienced as rupture. There was no transition, no shared attention, no bridge from one state to another. Activation spikes. The child does not have language for this, so they go still.

They learn something quietly:

Regulation can disappear without warning.

They also learn something else:

Big reactions make things worse.

So they get smaller.

Part II: The Teenager

Years later, the same person has learned how to stay quiet inside.

At home, safety has meant being small. Not drawing attention. Not escalating. Emotional states are kept tight, expressions muted. It works well enough in that environment.

It does not work with peers.

In groups, the unspoken rules are different. Visibility brings belonging. Intensity signals connection. The teenager watches others move easily between laughter, outrage, excitement. Their own internal world still feels large, but their expression remains narrow. They feel outside even when included.

Then they find a different group — kids who live closer to the edges. The ones who skip class together, talk back, test limits. The energy is higher. The rules looser. No one asks them to be smaller. The teen feels something unfamiliar: aliveness shared in real time.

Risk-taking becomes social glue. Sneaking out, breaking rules, trying substances. The first time they drink or smoke, the effect is not only chemical. The group gathers closer. Voices soften. Laughter comes easier. The internal tension drops in a way that feels both foreign and relieving.

They are not chasing oblivion. They are chasing regulation they never fully internalized.

The behavior stays mostly hidden. Secret. Manageable. It feels like something they can control, a bridge between the constricted self at home and the more animated self with peers.

The nervous system is still solving the same problem — now with different tools.

Part III: The Young Adult

The environment shifts again.

Friends scatter — jobs, schools, relationships, cities. The informal co-regulation of adolescence thins. Expectations increase. The young adult is now expected to function independently in systems that assume a level of internal stability they only partially possess.

They feel uncertain in ways they cannot explain. Others seem to move with confidence, while they move with careful observation. They second-guess their competence. Imposter feelings surface — not only intellectually, but physically, as tension, restlessness, and fatigue.

The old peer rituals — late nights, shared substances, collective intensity — are harder to maintain at the same scale. But the internal need remains. Alone in an apartment, in a dorm, in a new city, the familiar strategies resurface in more solitary form. A drink at night. Hours lost online. Rigid routines. Something predictable to hold the edges together.

It is not about pleasure. It is about coherence.

The child's screen, the teenager's peer rituals, and the young adult's solitary habits are variations on the same theme: the nervous system searching for containment in the absence of sufficiently internalized regulation.

The context changes. The strategy evolves. The problem remains the same.

Pause & Consider

Imagine the same earlier screentime moment unfolding differently.

A parent steps into the room and sits beside the child, placing a hand lightly on their shoulder.

"Hey sweetie, in five minutes we're going to turn this off and go eat. Let's find a good stopping point."

The child looks up. There is eye contact. A voice with rhythm. A body close enough to borrow from. The transition is no longer a rupture but a sequence shared between two nervous systems. Attention shifts gradually. Activation rises less sharply because it is met, not triggered alone.

On the surface, the difference seems minor — a few words, a change in tone, a pause before action.

Structurally, it is enormous.

In the first version, the child's regulation disappears without warning. In the second, regulation is transferred. The end of the activity is not simply enforced; it is navigated together. The child is not left alone with the spike in activation that comes with change. They are guided through it.

These are the moments where internal regulation is built — not through control, but through shared adjustment.

Addiction as Emotional Compression

Across the previous vignettes, the settings were different, the ages varied, and the behaviors took different forms. But the underlying problem remained consistent: the nervous system was managing more activation than it could safely discharge.

Addiction emerges in this context not as a single act or a sudden loss of control, but as a functional adaptation. It addresses a specific regulatory need.

One of its primary effects is to narrow the emotional field. When internal experience is chaotic, overwhelming, or diffuse, addiction channels attention into something focused and repeatable. The range of feeling contracts. Intensity becomes organized around the ritual rather than spilling outward in unpredictable ways. This narrowing can feel like relief, because the person is no longer facing the full, uncontained spectrum of internal states.

Addiction also creates predictability. In environments where emotional experience has been inconsistent or destabilizing, predictable sequences become deeply regulating. The time of day, the setting, the steps of the behavior — these form a structure the nervous system can anticipate. Anticipation itself becomes calming. The person knows what comes next, even if other parts of life feel uncertain.

Rhythm is another regulatory component. Repetition establishes a cadence: preparation, engagement, after-effect. This rhythm can substitute for the natural rhythms of co-regulated life — conversation, shared meals, collective decompression — that may be absent or insufficient. The ritual provides a pattern the body can follow when relational rhythms are unavailable.

Addiction also simulates control. When internal states feel unpredictable and external circumstances feel overwhelming, the ability to initiate a state change on demand can feel stabilizing. The person may not control the broader environment, but they can control this sequence. That sense of agency, even if limited, contributes to the behavior's regulatory power.

These features together illustrate a central function:

Addiction compresses unprocessed emotional load into a controllable ritual.

The grief that was never shared, the fear that was never metabolized, the shame that was never witnessed, the activation that never returned to baseline — these are not eliminated. They are condensed into a narrower, more manageable channel. The ritual becomes a container.

Seen from this perspective, addiction is a form of survival engineering. The nervous system is using the tools available to create stability under conditions of regulatory strain. The behavior may carry long-term costs, but its immediate function is not self-destruction. It is self-preservation under constraint.

This does not mean addiction is harmless, nor does it remove personal responsibility for behavior. But it shifts the frame from moral defect to adaptive strategy. Understanding the regulatory function of addiction clarifies why it persists despite consequences: it is solving a problem that has not yet been solved another way.

Across group-contained trauma, isolated trauma, and developmental dysregulation, the pattern is the same. When emotional load exceeds available relational regulation, the nervous system turns to repetitive, controllable behaviors to create containment. Addiction is one such behavior, shaped by environment, history, and opportunity, but rooted in the same structural need.

The question then becomes not only how to stop the behavior, but how to replace the containment it provided.

9.6

Stabilization vs. Integration

Understanding addiction as a regulatory strategy also clarifies why some recovery efforts help in important ways yet still leave something unresolved.

Many recovery systems provide elements that are immediately stabilizing. They offer structure — regular meetings, routines, and expectations that organize time and behavior. They emphasize repetition, which can be regulating in itself. They create belonging, often for people who recognize they feel isolated or misunderstood. They provide identity coherence, giving language and community around shared experience. For someone in acute dysregulation, these features can significantly reduce chaos. They can interrupt dangerous patterns, create accountability, and establish a predictable framework within which daily life becomes more manageable.

This phase is often essential. When a nervous system has been operating under high strain, stabilization can be lifesaving. Reducing immediate risk, establishing routine, and increasing social connection can lower the intensity of crisis and create enough space for the person to remain functional.

At the same time, stabilization is not the same as integration.

Some recovery environments, intentionally or not, rely heavily on mechanisms that continue to narrow emotional experience rather than expand the capacity to process it. Shame activation may be used as a behavioral control, keeping the person focused on their deficits or potential failure. Identity can become tightly organized around brokenness or pathology, which can provide coherence but also constrict the sense of self. Emotional expression may remain bounded within certain acceptable forms, while deeper or more complex states are still difficult to metabolize in relationship.

In these cases, the substance or behavior may be removed, but the underlying regulatory pattern remains similar. Emotional load is still managed through compression — now through identity, vigilance about relapse, or fear of moral failure rather than through the original addictive behavior. The system is more stable, but it may still be operating under contraction.

The distinction can be framed simply:

Stabilization reduces chaos. Integration restores regulation.

Stabilization helps the person stop falling apart. Integration helps the nervous system learn that it does not have to hold itself together through constant constriction. Integration involves experiences of safety where emotional states can rise and fall without overwhelming the system and without being forced into narrow channels of control.

Addiction is not fully healed when the behavior stops if the nervous system still relies on contraction as its primary means of regulation. Healing deepens when safety is experienced in ways that allow for expansion — broader emotional range, flexible identity, and the ability to remain connected to others without suppressing internal experience.

This perspective does not dismiss the value of recovery systems that emphasize structure and belonging. Rather, it highlights a further step. Once immediate stabilization is achieved, the work of integration begins: building internal and relational capacities that make ongoing compression unnecessary.

In this sense, recovery involves more than abstinence. It involves helping the nervous system experience safety without contraction.

9.7

Why This Matters

When addiction is understood through the lens of nervous system regulation, its persistence begins to make sense in a new way.

Across the situations described in this chapter, the same physiological pattern appears. When emotional load is carried without sufficient relational buffering, the nervous system must find ways to contain activation on its own. Under conditions of regulatory isolation, addiction is not anomalous — it is predictable. The greater the burden placed on an individual system to manage threat, grief, shame, or chronic stress without shared regulation, the more likely it is to rely on repetitive, controllable behaviors to narrow internal experience.

Developmental history shapes this vulnerability. Nervous systems that matured without consistent co-regulation often enter adulthood with partial internal regulatory architecture. They may function well in many domains, yet remain highly sensitive to overload. When later stressors occur — loss, trauma, transition, isolation — the system can become destabilized more quickly, not because of weakness, but because it is working with limited internal resources for returning to baseline.

The inverse is also true. When regulation is shared — through safe connection, recognition, and relational stability — the nervous system does not need to compress emotional load into solitary rituals as intensely. Activation can rise and fall within relationship. Emotional states can be metabolized rather than contained through contraction. The pressure on any one behavior to serve as the primary regulator decreases.

These patterns point toward a central conclusion:

Addiction is not evidence of weak character. It is evidence of a nervous system forced to regulate without sufficient help.

This reframing does not remove responsibility for behavior or its consequences. Instead, it directs attention to where meaningful change must occur. If addiction functions as a regulatory substitute, then healing requires more than eliminating the behavior. It requires restoring conditions in which the nervous system can experience safety, discharge activation, and develop broader regulatory capacity.

This shift leads directly into the next question. If addictive rituals once provided containment under strain, what forms of ritual can support regulation without contraction? How can structure, repetition, and shared experience be used to help the nervous system expand safely rather than narrow itself to survive?

The next chapter explores this transition — from survival-based containment to restorative regulation.

Chapter 10 - Ritual That Restores

Addiction isn't just about compulsion. It's about rhythm.

Every addictive pattern, no matter how destructive, had a rhythm to it — a predictable loop that created just enough structure to feel like safety. It marked time. It signaled transitions. It gave shape to the in-between. And when that pattern is removed, what's left isn't just absence. It's a void of structure. A life with no tempo.

This is why healing can feel hollow at first. Not because recovery isn't working, but because the ritual is gone. And ritual, even in its most distorted forms, was doing something important. It was *holding you* when nothing else did. It was wrapping your day in predictability, even if the outcome was painful.

What comes next is not about finding a replacement — it's about learning how to build *restorative rituals* that hold your life in new ways. Not to manage you. Not to keep you in line. But to give shape to the parts of you that are learning how to stay present, connected, and whole.

Restorative ritual is different from routine. Routine is what you do. Ritual is how you do it — and *why*. It's the meaning embedded in repetition. The reverence in the ordinary. It doesn't need to be dramatic or spiritual or even particularly noticeable to others. It just needs to speak to something inside you that craves rhythm without rigidity. Intention without perfection.

This chapter is about finding those rituals. Not through prescriptions or formulas, but through exploration. What makes your breath deepen? What makes your thoughts quiet? What helps you return to your body when shame tries to drag you out of it?

Ritual that restores isn't about becoming a better version of yourself.
It's about building a life that feels safe enough that you don't have to perform.

It's about rhythm that holds.
Ritual that reflects.
And patterns that return you — not to addiction — but to yourself.

10.1

Rebuilding Rhythm

In the early stages of recovery, life can feel strangely formless. The spiral, for all its damage, had a rhythm. It offered predictability — even if what you were predicting was pain. There was a script. A loop. A set of known variables that told your body, *this is what happens next*. When that pattern ends, what follows isn't just peace. It's silence. And for many, that silence is unbearable.

This is why relapse often has nothing to do with craving and everything to do with timing. There's no structure. No rhythm. The day stretches open and unmarked, and the body starts reaching — not for the substance, necessarily, but for something to hold it in place.

Ritual isn't about discipline. It's about orientation. It's about knowing where you are in your own life. Addiction used to offer that orientation. Now, it's up to you to rebuild it — not with punishment or rigid structure, but with intentional rhythm.

Rebuilding rhythm starts small. It's not about routines that look good on paper. It's about sensory memory — actions that help the body remember it's safe. It might be lighting a candle each morning. Taking a short walk at the same time every day. Touching your own hand. Naming your intention aloud before you open your computer. Closing the day with a few lines of reflection, not for performance, but for presence.

None of these rituals need to be perfect or profound. They only need to be *predictable*. Enough that your body can begin to recognize the rhythm and settle into it. Enough that time begins to feel shaped again, not endless. Enough that you start to experience yourself *as someone who can create safety on purpose.*

You don't need to map your whole day. You just need a few touchpoints. A few repetitions that signal: *I am here. I am allowed to take up space. I do not need to spiral to feel real.*

Rhythm isn't a replacement for addiction. It's an invitation to return. Not to the past — but to the self you've been too scattered, too numb, or too afraid to inhabit fully. And each time you choose a ritual that aligns with that return — no matter how small — you are participating in healing. Not as a task, but as a rhythm.

10.2

Meaning, Not Management

In the aftermath of addiction, it's easy to crave structure — not as a tool for growth, but as a shield against the chaos that came before. When the spiral stops, the instinct to impose order can feel like safety. We download productivity apps, we build color-coded schedules, we start tracking every moment as if recovery is a performance review. We tell ourselves that discipline is healing — that if we just manage well enough, we'll never slip again.

But management isn't healing. It's another form of control. It keeps the outer world tidy while the inner world remains unsupervised. Rigid routines and hyper-efficiency may look like progress, but often, they're just the next mask. You're no longer spiraling — but you're still bracing. Still performing. Still afraid of what happens if the structure breaks.

This is where the difference between routine and ritual matters.

Routines are about output. Rituals are about relationship. A routine gets things done. A ritual, however simple, helps you return to yourself. The same behavior can fall into either category. Drinking a cup of tea because it's part of your checklist is routine. Drinking a cup of tea because you need stillness, warmth, breath — that's ritual. The action is the same. The meaning is entirely different.

Meaningful rituals don't manage you. They hold you. They don't rush you into performance or demand that you accomplish anything. They simply ask: *Did this help me come home to myself?* And if it did, then it matters. Even if it was brief. Even if no one else noticed. Even if it looked like nothing.

For many in recovery, the temptation is to replace the addictive pattern with something equally compulsive — hyper-clean eating, excessive exercise, nonstop productivity. These new routines feel safe at first. But soon, they become conditions for worthiness. They become new metrics to fail by. And they erase the possibility of rest.

Rituals that restore don't work that way. They're built on relationship — not results. They don't require you to be efficient or emotionally clean. They just require presence. A moment of intention. A quiet acknowledgement that *this is for me, and I am allowed to have it.*

That might mean closing your laptop at the same time each night to remind yourself that work does not define you. It might mean stepping outside each morning to feel the air and remember that the world is still turning. It might mean folding your clothes with care not because you're chasing order, but because you're practicing tenderness. These small repetitions become your way back to coherence. Not productivity. Not perfection. Just coherence.

Addiction removed meaning from behavior — it turned everything automatic. Ritual brings meaning back. It reintroduces you to your own needs, not through grand gestures, but through daily acts of witnessing. And when you build those acts with intention, you stop trying to manage yourself into healing. You start living into it instead.

10.3

Witnessing, Not Performing

Many people recovering from addiction struggle with being seen. Not because they don't want to be known — but because so often, being seen meant being judged, misunderstood, or required to prove something. For some, being visible came only through performance. For others, it led to punishment. Either way, the result was the same: safety became linked with invisibility.

That association is hard to break. Even in recovery, it can linger beneath the surface. You start building rituals — small, steady ones that feel honest — but the moment someone else is present, the dynamic shifts. Suddenly it feels like a performance. Like you're being evaluated. And the moment that happens, the ritual loses its center. You're no longer grounding. You're managing someone else's perception of you.

But being witnessed isn't the same as being watched. And presence doesn't have to mean performance.

Witnessing is about connection, not evaluation. It's about someone sitting beside you, not above you. It's about having your experience mirrored back to you with gentleness, not critique. And most importantly, it's about someone being there *without needing you to be impressive, put together, or better than you are.*

Rituals that include others — even in subtle ways — can be some of the most restorative. Sharing a morning walk. Preparing a meal side by side. Ending a conversation with the same phrase every time, like "You're still here, and I'm grateful." These repetitions don't just build rhythm. They build relationship. They allow both people to show up, not as roles, but as selves.

But for that to happen, the space has to be safe. That means clear boundaries. It means mutual respect. It means checking your impulse to prove your progress or manage someone else's emotions. And sometimes, it means saying aloud: *This is for me. You're welcome to be here, but you don't get to define it.*

You may not be ready to share your rituals with others right away. That's okay. Start by witnessing yourself. Start by being present for the small things — the cup of tea, the journal page, the ten minutes of quiet — and naming them

194

as real. Not tasks. Not evidence of recovery. Just *truths in motion.*

You don't have to make healing performative in order for it to count.

You don't have to do it alone to make it real.

You just need to be witnessed — not managed, not measured — and to allow that presence to affirm something you've been trying to believe all along:

That you are worthy of love without needing to earn it.

10.4

Relational Ritual and Coherence

Healing often begins alone — but it cannot stay there.

No matter how grounded your personal rituals become, they are still shaped by the context around you. You may learn to hold your own breath, to steady your hands, to return to yourself in quiet — but eventually, you'll be asked to bring that self into relationship. And when that happens, the old stories resurface. The ones that told you your needs were a burden. That your feelings made things worse. That connection was conditional, and love always came with a ledger.

It's easy, after that kind of history, to believe that safety means solitude. That the only way to stay whole is to stay alone. But the nervous system tells a different story. It softens in presence. It anchors through eye contact, proximity, attunement. You may have learned to numb or dissociate, but your body has always wanted rhythm — not just from within, but from others.

This is where relational ritual becomes vital.

Relational rituals aren't grand declarations. They're small, repeated acts that remind you — and those you're close to — that *you are allowed to show up here, fully and consistently.* A check-in before the day begins. A question you always ask each other at the end of a hard one. A standing invitation to walk, to sit, to pause together without fixing. These rituals offer more than habit. They create a sense of coherence — where the emotional logic of being together starts to make sense again.

For some, especially those who've been deeply hurt in relationships, this can feel like too much. Sharing space, even quietly, can feel like surrender. Letting someone witness your rhythm can feel like exposure. That's okay. Go slowly. But do go. Because the alternative — a life entirely managed in isolation — may feel safer, but it rarely leads to integration.

Coherence in relationship means your inner world can be reflected outward, and the reflection doesn't shatter you. It means you're no longer shape-shifting to stay loved, or collapsing to stay seen. It means your rituals aren't just survival tools — they become invitations. Ways to say: *This is how I live now. Would you like to meet me here?*

This is especially powerful in chosen family, partnerships, and recovery circles. When shared rituals are born from mutual trust, not obligation, they become scaffolding — not cages. You don't need to have the same routines. You just need enough rhythm to return to each other. Enough repetition to remind both nervous systems: *We're still here. And we don't have to disappear to stay connected.*

When coherence enters a relationship, recovery stops being a solo pursuit. It becomes a shared experience of returning — again and again — without shame.

Not because everything is easy.
But because the rhythm holds, even when you don't.

10.5

Returning Without Replacing

In early recovery, there's a quiet but seductive temptation: to find something that will take the old pattern's place. Something healthy. Something productive. Something that still gives you that feeling of *anchoring*, but without the guilt, secrecy, or shame. And often, that search is praised. Encouraged. Even applauded.

You stop drinking, and you start running.
You leave the spiral of compulsive relationships, and you dive into work.
You give up one rigid control — and unconsciously adopt another.

It's not intentional. It's not always visible. But it's common. And it makes sense.

Because when the pattern ends, the structure goes with it. The rhythm, however painful, leaves a silence. And without meaningfully engaging with that silence, we often rush to fill it — with anything that makes us feel okay again. Safe. Regulated. Real.

But the truth is:

Recovery isn't about substitution. It's about reclamation.
It's about learning not to *replace* the ritual, but to return to the space it left behind with intention. With presence. With a willingness to ask: *What was I hoping this behavior*

would hold for me? What did it let me feel — or avoid feeling? And what can I build now that speaks to that same need without erasing who I am in the process?

This is not the same as discipline. This is discernment.

Because even the most "healthy" behaviors can become distorted if they're used to outrun pain. Fitness. Spirituality. Hustle. Minimalism. Even recovery itself can become performative if it's just another identity we wear to avoid being witnessed in our vulnerability.

That's why returning matters more than replacing.
Returning to the moment.
Returning to the body.
Returning to the breath, the intention, the feeling — not because it's easy, but because it's honest.

The goal isn't to never reach. The goal is to understand what you're reaching for — and to have more than one way to meet that need. The old rituals weren't failures. They were strategies. But you are allowed to build new ones now. Ones that hold you, not manage you. Ones that reflect your humanity, not your fear.

And maybe most importantly — ones that don't disappear the moment you stop performing.

Vignette: The Second Cup

He used to wake up with panic in his throat. Not because anything was wrong — but because he didn't know what to do without the chaos. Mornings used to start with adrenaline: missed alarms, empty bottles, stale breath, guilt already coiled behind his ribs before his feet hit the floor. Now, it was quiet. Clean. Still.

Too still.

For the first few months, he treated recovery like a job. Lists. Schedules. Weekly progress reports in his head. Gym, group, groceries. He replaced drinking with running. Replaced sex with spreadsheets. Woke up at 5:30 because it made him feel accomplished. Went to bed with audiobooks because silence still scared him. Everyone called him disciplined. He called it momentum. But deep down, he knew it wasn't healing. It was just *management* with a better PR team.

Then one morning — mid-winter, light barely cracking the horizon — he made a second cup of tea.

The first had gone cold while he answered emails. Nothing unusual. But this time, instead of rushing into the next task, he stood in the kitchen and made another cup. Slowly. On purpose. No goal. No box to check. He stirred the honey longer than needed. Let the steam hit his face. Breathed in a full floral palate of aromas that teased his tastebuds. Didn't look at his phone.

It was five quiet minutes. And for reasons he couldn't quite explain, he cried the whole time.

That became his ritual.

Not every day. Not with ceremony. Just sometimes — when the house was quiet, and he could remember that stillness didn't mean emptiness. That a moment could be gentle without being earned. He started leaving space between things: a breath between meetings, a full pause before responding to texts, a few minutes on the porch with nothing but the sky for company.

He told no one at first. It felt too fragile to explain.

Later, he shared it with someone in his recovery group. A man who used to drink alone every night and now took long evening walks by himself just to listen to the wind through trees. "That's your second cup," he said. And they both laughed — but softly, like it mattered.

Eventually, the ritual grew. Not in complexity, but in context. His partner started joining him on some mornings. They didn't talk much. Sometimes just sat across from one another, mugs warm in their hands, the silence no longer a threat but a kind of trust. On harder days, he would text a friend and say: *I'm off. Can we share five minutes of quiet later?* Not to fix anything. Just to not be alone in the ache.

He stopped measuring progress by how "good" he was doing. He started asking instead: *Where am I today? Do I need rhythm? Or rest? Witnessing? Or solitude?* The answers shifted. He let them.

Once, in early recovery, he thought he'd never feel normal again. That he'd always be patching together some version of stability out of broken pieces. Now, he knew better. The pieces weren't broken — they were just honest. And they didn't need to be managed. They just needed room.

Sometimes he still slipped — not into drinking, but into perfectionism. Into control. Into silence that wasn't chosen. But now, he had a way back. A rhythm.

Sometimes, it was the second cup.

Sometimes, it was asking for a walk.

Sometimes, it was just one hand over his heart, saying nothing at all.

But each time, he returned.

Not to the old pattern.

To himself.

"*The meaning of life is just to be alive. It is so plain and so obvious and so simple. And yet, everybody rushes around in a great panic as if it were necessary to achieve something beyond themselves.*"
— Alan Watts, *The Culture of Counter-Culture*

Part IV - For the Witness

Healing doesn't happen in isolation.
And neither does collapse.

For every person in crisis, there is someone watching.
A parent. A partner. A friend. A child. A therapist. A
stranger in the right place at the right time.
Sometimes they stay. Sometimes they flee. Sometimes they
try so hard to help that they forget to *hold*.

This part of the book is for them.

For the people who want to show up but don't know how.
For the people who stayed and got it wrong.
For the people who are trying to love someone through
something that doesn't follow logic or timelines.

You don't have to fix them.
You don't have to say the perfect thing.
You just have to stop asking them to be okay before
they're allowed to be loved.

Witnessing isn't a passive act. It's an offering. A quiet
bravery. A promise that says:
You don't have to disappear in order to be safe with me.

Let's begin.

Chapter 11 - To Love Someone Through Collapse

This chapter is not about fixing anyone.

It's not a roadmap. It's not a script. It's not a guide for walking someone else to safety while avoiding your own discomfort. If anything, it's an invitation to let go of the belief that healing must always look like progress — or that your role is to pull someone through their spiral before they're ready to stand.

Because collapse doesn't follow a schedule. It doesn't happen cleanly. And it rarely resolves in ways that make sense from the outside.

To love someone through collapse is to love them without asking them to perform. To choose relationship over reassurance. To sit beside someone who is coming undone and not interpret that undoing as a personal failure, or a problem to solve.

This is harder than it sounds.

Most of us are taught to comfort, to redirect, to reframe. We say things like "At least…" or "Try to think positive," not because we're cruel, but because we're scared. Scared of saying the wrong thing. Scared of witnessing pain we can't fix. Scared of what their spiral might reflect back to us about our own capacity to fall apart.

But collapse, when held properly, is not the end. It is the beginning of truth. Of repair. Of honesty. So raw it cannot be faked. And if you are someone who has been asked to stay during that process — not to steer it, not to shortcut it, but to stay — then what's being asked of you is sacred.

You will be tempted to offer advice when what's needed is presence.

You will be tempted to interpret their behavior through your own lens.

You will want to say the right thing. But sometimes, the right thing is silence, with your hand on their shoulder and your breath in rhythm with theirs.

Loving someone through collapse does not mean tolerating harm. It doesn't mean excusing abuse or neglect. It means being honest about boundaries while remaining committed to connection. It means refusing to let their spiral isolate them further — not by dragging them out of it, but by making sure they know they're not alone in it.

You are not their savior.

You are not their recovery.

You are the witness. The tether. The safe place to land.

And sometimes, that's the most powerful role of all.

11.1

What Not to Say (and Why)

When someone you care about is collapsing — emotionally, behaviorally, spiritually — it's natural to want to say something that helps. Most of us weren't taught how to sit with pain, so we reach for reassurance. For hope. For control. We try to lighten the moment, shift the perspective, smooth over the discomfort with something *helpful.*

But collapse doesn't need help. It needs holding. And many of the things we're conditioned to say in the name of comfort actually create more distance.

Here are some of the most common phrases — and why they often do more harm than good:

"At least…"

"At least you're still here." "At least it wasn't worse." "At least you have your health."

These statements are usually meant to inspire perspective. But to someone in collapse, they feel dismissive. They bypass the present reality in favor of imagined gratitude. They say: *Your pain is only valid if someone else has it worse.*

"Everything happens for a reason."

In moments of profound distress, this phrase can feel like gaslighting. It suggests that suffering is part of a grand design — a comfort only when the person is ready to hear it, and devastating when they're not. More often than not, it relieves the speaker of discomfort without addressing the pain at hand.

"You're strong." / "You'll get through this."

These statements can feel uplifting on the surface, but they often land as expectations. They tell the person how they *should* respond, rather than making room for how they *actually* feel. Being told you're strong when you feel like you're breaking can feel like a command to hide your collapse.

"Let me know if you need anything."

This one comes from kindness — and fear. It's a way of signaling support while placing the burden of asking back on the person who's already overwhelmed. In moments of collapse, most people can't articulate what they need. They need presence, not permission to reach out.

"You just have to stay positive."

Positivity has its place. But collapse isn't about attitude —

it's about emotional overwhelm, nervous system depletion, and often years of suppressed pain coming to the surface. When we ask someone to "stay positive," what we're often really asking is: *Please don't make me feel this, too.*

What's more powerful than any of these phrases is something much simpler — and rarer.

Try:

- "I'm here."
- "You don't have to explain it."
- "I'm not going anywhere."
- "You don't need to be okay for me to care."
- "Can I sit with you in this?"

Because the truth is, words aren't what hold people together. **Presence does.**

And when presence comes without pressure, shame begins to dissolve.

You don't need the perfect thing to say.

You just need to stay close enough that they don't have to go through it alone.

Pause and Consider

If someone you care about is collapsing, you may feel helpless. You may want to do something — anything — to ease their pain, to pull them back, to make things normal again. But pause with that urge for a moment.

Ask yourself:
– What part of *their* pain is touching something in *me*?
– Am I trying to help them — or am I trying to silence my own discomfort?
– What would it mean to offer support without needing to be the solution?

You're allowed to feel overwhelmed. You're allowed to be scared. And still, you can choose to stay.
You don't need to have the answers. You don't need to say the perfect thing.

Your role isn't to rescue.
Your role is to *remain*.

Sit beside them.
Let them unravel without rushing them back into coherence.
Let your love be quiet enough that they can hear their own voice again.

And remember: the most healing thing you can say might be the simplest —
"You don't have to go through this alone."

11.2

How to Hold Without Fixing

Holding someone through collapse doesn't mean staying silent. It doesn't mean being passive or stepping back completely. But it *does* mean letting go of the idea that your job is to solve the spiral, speed it up, or make it more palatable. Fixing is fast. Holding is slow.

And slow is often what healing needs.

To hold someone is to offer structure without demand. It means showing up consistently, with softness, even when things get messy. Especially then. It means listening with the intent to understand — not to analyze, redirect, or cheerlead. When someone is unraveling, what they need most is not your insight. It's your steadiness.

That starts with regulating yourself.

When someone you love is in pain, your nervous system will respond. You may feel the urge to talk them out of their sadness, to explain their fear away, to prove that everything is fine. But more often than not, that impulse is about *you* — about wanting relief from the discomfort of witnessing someone you love hurt in a way you can't control.

Holding means noticing that impulse — and staying anyway.

It might look like staying on the phone while they cry without rushing to offer solutions. It might look like texting, *"I'm thinking of you,"* without asking how they're doing when they're clearly overwhelmed. It might mean sitting beside them and saying nothing — not because you don't care, but because your presence says everything they need to hear.

Holding without fixing also means honoring their timeline.
Their healing might not look the way you expected.
They may not respond how you hoped.
They may be angry, withdrawn, numb, or contradictory.
They may come undone in ways that test your own boundaries.

Your job isn't to absorb them.
Your job is to stay clear and present — without disappearing, without controlling, and without needing to be the hero.

If you don't know what to do, try saying that.
"I don't know what you need right now, but I'm here."
"I'm not going to rush you."
"This is hard, and I'm not afraid of it."

Sometimes the most powerful thing you can give someone is the freedom to fall apart *in front of you* without fear that you'll leave — or that you'll ask them to be okay before they're ready.

To hold someone is not to keep them from breaking.
It's to help them trust that breaking is not the end of being loved.

10.3

The Risk of Loving Someone Who May Not Heal

There is no guarantee that the person you love will make it through this.

That's not something most books about healing say out loud. We like stories with arcs. We want redemption, resolution, recovery. We want to believe that if we show up well enough — if we say the right things, offer the right support, love them the right way — then they'll choose the light. They'll get better. They'll come back.

But not everyone does.

Not everyone wants to.
Not everyone can.
And not everyone sees healing the way you do.

Loving someone in collapse comes with risk. Not just the risk that they may never heal, but the quieter risk that you'll lose yourself trying to make them okay. That you'll stay too long in the name of hope, silence your own needs in the name of patience, and begin to confuse love with endurance.

Sometimes, the person you love won't choose the path. They'll choose the pattern.
They'll rewrite the truth.
They'll find ways to keep spiraling, even while telling you they want to change.

And that's when the hardest kind of love is required: the kind with boundaries.

Not ultimatums. Not punishment. But clarity. The kind that says: *I will walk with you — but I will not walk into the fire for you. I will hold space — but I will not disappear inside it. I love you — but I will not abandon myself to prove it.*

This isn't giving up. It's grieving honestly.

Because when you accept that someone may not heal — or may not heal in the way or timeline you hoped — you stop waiting for the version of them you imagined. And you start seeing the person who's actually here. Their limits. Their choices. Their humanity.

That doesn't mean you stop loving them.

It means you stop trading your wholeness for their potential.

This kind of love is quiet. It's not dramatic. It doesn't make for big declarations or final scenes. But it's the kind of love that allows both people to remain intact — even if one never finds their way out.

Sometimes the most radical thing you can do is love someone exactly as they are — and still choose not to follow them where they're going.

Not every story ends in healing.
But every story deserves the dignity of truth.

Pause and Consider

Most healing stories end with a return. A redemption arc. The person makes it through. The support was worth it. The love worked.

But not every story resolves like that — and if you've been loving someone who may not choose to heal, you know this ache. You've hoped. You've waited. You've tried everything. And still, they remain in the spiral, or drift further away. Maybe they don't see the problem. Maybe they do, and don't know how to face it. Maybe they say they're trying, but the change never comes.

If you've been loving like your life depends on it — if you've been measuring your worth by how well you can *rescue* someone else — this is where the story turns.

This book may have felt like it was for them. But maybe, quietly, it was always for you.

Re-read the pages you thought were theirs.
Sit with the questions you thought they needed to answer.
Ask yourself:
– What part of me believed I had to earn love through fixing?
– When did I start confusing proximity to pain with purpose?
– Who was I before I became the strong one? The reliable one? The one who never breaks?

You are not responsible for someone else's healing.
You are responsible for how long you stay in a role that asks you to disappear.

There is nothing selfish about choosing to come home to yourself.

And there is no failure in recognizing that someone else's story is not your redemption.

11.4

When They Do Choose Healing

Sometimes, they do choose it.

Not all at once. Not with fanfare. But slowly. Unevenly. With hesitation and false starts and long silences that suddenly end with, *"I think I'm ready."*

And when it happens — when someone you love starts reaching back toward life, toward themselves — your instinct might be to cheer, to plan, to pull them forward into the future you always hoped for. But healing doesn't work like that. Choosing healing is not the end of collapse. It's the beginning of learning to live differently. And it will take more from both of you than you might expect.

They may still be fragile. Angry. Quiet. Lost in grief. They may not know how to talk about what they're feeling. They may bounce between moments of connection and days of retreat. You'll wonder if they're slipping. You'll want to ask. You'll want to *do something*.

But what they need most isn't your enthusiasm. It's your steadiness.

When someone chooses healing, what they're really choosing is to begin again — *without the ritual that once made them feel whole.* That means they're raw. Exposed. Learning how to tolerate their own truth without anesthetic. What they need is someone who doesn't rush their process, or wrap it in unrealistic hope.

They need someone who can say:

- *"You don't need to impress me."*
- *"I'm not going to keep score."*
- *"We can go slow."*

- *"You don't owe me progress — just honesty."*
- *"Your self-love is beautiful!"*

Healing isn't linear. They will falter. They may relapse — not always into behavior, but into belief: that they're too much. That it's too late. That they've already disappointed you. That this moment of return won't last.

That's where your presence matters most.

Not to rescue. Not to parent. But to mirror back to them the quiet, steady truth: *You're still here. And I still see you.*

If they invite you in, show up — not with advice, but with curiosity. Not with demands for change, but with a willingness to build rituals together that honor their unfolding self. Healing doesn't always mean going back to the way things were. Sometimes it means starting a new relationship — even with the same person.

To love someone who chooses healing is to let them write their own arc — and to be grateful, every day, that you get to be there as they do.

Because they're not just coming back to life.

They're coming back to *themselves.*

And your presence, without pressure, might be part of what helps them stay.

Closing

You Were Never the Problem

You made it here.

Maybe slowly. Maybe with breaks. Maybe through tears or silence or disbelief. But you stayed. And staying is its own kind of healing.

If you've seen yourself in these pages — in the collapse, in the ritual, in the ache for coherence — know this:
You were never broken.
You were never too much.
You were never the problem.

You were adapting. Surviving. Finding rhythm in the wreckage. You were building systems of meaning in a world that rarely paused long enough to offer you a soft place to land.

Addiction, for many, was the first system that made sense. The first ritual that held. The first time something answered the chaos inside with a reliable script. Letting that go — or even just seeing it clearly — takes courage most people never speak about. But you did that. Are doing that. Even now.

If you came to this book trying to understand someone you love, I hope you found more than explanations. I hope you found *yourself.* I hope you learned that love is not rescue. That presence is not performance. And that your job was never to fix what someone else refused to feel.

And if you came here looking for your own way out — or your own way in — I hope you found language for the parts of you that don't usually get named. The patterns. The grief. The longing. The strength you didn't know was strength because it never looked the way you were told it should.

You don't need to become someone else.

You just need space to become someone *true*.

Let go of the shame that told you healing had to look a certain way. Let go of the guilt that said if you had done it "right," you'd already be whole. Let go of the timelines, the milestones, the metrics.

You are allowed to build a life slowly.
You are allowed to begin again — as many times as it takes.

And you are allowed to build that life in rhythm with people who don't ask you to be smaller, softer, simpler, or stronger than you really are.

This isn't the end.

It's just the first time someone looked you in the eye and said:

You are not the problem.
You never were.
And now, you get to come home.

Resources and Support

You don't have to do this alone.

If this book stirred something in you — if it unearthed grief, recognition, fear, or hope — let that be a sign that your nervous system is ready for something new. But you don't have to figure it out by yourself.

Healing begins with presence. And sometimes, presence starts with reaching out.

If you are in immediate crisis

Please contact a local crisis line or seek support at any of the following:

- **988 Suicide & Crisis Lifeline** (U.S.): Call or text 988 or visit 988lifeline.org

- **Crisis Text Line** (U.S., U.K., Canada): Text HOME to 741741

- **RAINN (Rape, Abuse & Incest National Network):** 1-800-656-HOPE or rainn.org

- **SAMHSA National Helpline:** 1-800-662-HELP (4357) – free, confidential treatment referral and information service for individuals and families facing mental and/or substance use disorders

If you are seeking therapeutic support

- Look for a trauma-informed therapist or counselor familiar with addiction recovery, grief, codependency, or emotional regulation

- Explore directories such as psychologytoday.com or inclusivetherapists.com

- Ask for support groups that honor both traditional and alternative recovery paths (not all healing happens in 12 steps)

If you are a loved one supporting someone in collapse

- Consider attending **Al-Anon, CoDA (Codependents Anonymous),** or other support spaces for families, partners, and friends
- Read books like *Codependent No More* by Melody Beattie or *It Didn't Start With You* by Mark Wolynn
- Seek peer support where your feelings can be processed without shame

If you are rebuilding ritual and coherence

- Journal. Start small. Name what hurts and what helps. Let your voice come home.
- Build daily rhythms that include your body: walks, tea, stretching, quiet breath.
- Share space with people who don't require performance — even one person is enough.

Remember:

Healing doesn't ask you to become someone new.
It asks you to **stop pretending you were ever broken.**

Wherever you are in the process, there is room for you here.
And wherever you go next — you don't have to arrive perfectly.

You just have to arrive.